# ⊗ INSIGHT GUIDES

# NEW YORK
## shoppingguide

**Dıscovery**
CHANNEL

**APA PUBLICATIONS** L
Part of the Langenscheidt Publishing Group

**Right**: the stylish interior of a chic jewelry store in Nolita.

# Introduction

# Contents

# Areas

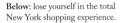

**Below**: lose yourself in the total New York shopping experience.

## Maps

*Inside Front Cover:*
*  New York*
*Inside Back Cover:*
*  New York Subways*

*For individual zone maps,*
*see area chapters*

## Features

**Below**: window shopping
offers lots of temptation.

## Directory

# New York Shopping

New York is one of the world's great shopping cities. There is something for everyone here: glamorous department stores, exclusive boutiques, gargantuan bookstores, a vast range of specialty and cheap outlet stores. Such a bewildering array of possibilities calls for guidance. This *New York Shopping Guide*, with its careful selection of stores, expert information, and handbag-friendly format, helps you make an informed choice.

The guide divides the city into ten areas, nine in Manhattan and one in Brooklyn. The selection of shopping venues are then listed by type: Fashion & Footwear, Design & Interior, Childrens, etc. Each shop is cross-referenced to an area map (in square brackets following the address). Where there is more than one branch of a shop in Manhattan, we have usually described the main or flagship store. The addresses of other branches are provided unless there are more than three in the city, in which case please look on the website for the other locations.

Alongside the main listings are practical tips, background information, and ideas on where to go when you need a break from the shops. Features on notable aspects of New York's shopping scene are also interspersed throughout the book. At the end of the guide you'll find a directory, containing essential information on transport, money matters, tipping, sales, and more. There's also an A–Z listing of all the shops featured. This guide was written by long-time New York resident, author, and shopping expert Amy Richards.

## Size chart

### Women's Dresses/Suits

| US | Continental | UK |
|----|-------------|-----|
| 6 | 38/34N | 8/30 |
| 8 | 40/36N | 10/32 |
| 10 | 42/38N | 12/34 |
| 12 | 44/40N | 14/36 |
| 14 | 46/42N | 16/38 |
| 16 | 48/44N | 18/40 |

### Women's Shoes

| US | Continental | UK |
|----|-------------|-----|
| 4½ | 36 | 3 |
| 5½ | 37 | 4 |
| 6½ | 38 | 5 |
| 7½ | 39 | 6 |
| 8½ | 40 | 7 |
| 9½ | 41 | 8 |
| 10½ | 42 | 9 |

### Men's Shirts

| US | Continental | UK |
|----|-------------|-----|
| 14 | 36 | 14 |
| 14½ | 37 | 14½ |
| 15 | 38 | 15 |
| 15½ | 39 | 15½ |
| 16 | 40 | 16 |
| 16½ | 41 | 16½ |
| 17 | 42 | 17 |

### Men's Suits

| US | Continental | UK |
|----|-------------|-----|
| 34 | 44 | 34 |
| — | 46 | 36 |
| 38 | 48 | 38 |
| — | 50 | 40 |
| 42 | 52 | 42 |
| — | 54 | 44 |
| 46 | 56 | 46 |

### Men's Shoes

| US | Continental | UK |
|----|-------------|-----|
| 6½ | — | 6 |
| 7½ | 40 | 7 |
| 8½ | 41 | 8 |
| 9½ | 42 | 9 |
| 10½ | 43 | 10 |
| 11½ | 44 | 11 |

▼ **FAO Schwarz** *767 Fifth Avenue, Midtown [p24].* A spectacular shopping experience for children. Life-sized toy animals and a Barbie nursery will keep most children contented for a while.

■ **Strand Bookstore** *828 Broadway, Greenwich Village [p77].* America's largest secondhand bookstore, with 2½ million books, from bargain remainders to $100,000 rarities.

■ **Takashimaya** *693 Fifth Avenue, Midtown [p22].* A different kind of department store, with works of art amidst the clothing and leather goods. Extravagant and very Japanese.

■ **B&H Photo-Video** *420 Ninth Avenue, Flatiron [p54].* Professionals and amateurs are catered to at this photography store, which sells all kinds of equipment the photographer could need. The store adheres to a strict Orthodox Jewish religious calendar.

■ **Macy's** *141 West 34th Street, Midtown [p22].* Taking up an entire city block, the largest department store in the world is a New York institution.

■ **J&R** *23 Park Row, Tribeca/Downtown [p107].* J&R is a block full of electronics – and is really many stores in one, providing a great choice and a chance to bargain.

▶ **Bergdorf Goodman** *754 Fifth Avenue, Midtown [p21].* The most traditional of New York's department stores, with seven floors of women's clothes, shoes, jewelry, and beauty products. 'Gentlemen' are catered for across the street.

▲ **Zabar's Gourmet Foods** *2245 Broadway, Upper West Side [p46].* Famous for their selection of gourmet foods. Eat like a king – or take home for an impressive gift.

■ **C.O. Bigelow Apothecaries** *414 Sixth Avenue, Greenwich Village [p75].* Grand old-style pharmacy, selling everything from homeopathic remedies to imported toothpaste.

▼ **ABC Carpet & Home** *888 Broadway, Flatiron [p53].* Two stores side-by-side one offering sumptuous carpets and rugs, the other vases, lamps, and furniture – some new, some antique – in a rich and colorful display. Beautiful things for your own home or to give as gifts.

# INTRODUCING NEW YORK

*It's otherwise known as shop-happy New York, where everything is up for grabs and you can get it wholesale, retail, or any which way you choose*

**N**ew York City – the proverbial shopping capital of the world – is North America's biggest urban center. Its location gives this particular metropolis a panache all of its own among the states of the Union, a port of entry remarkably cohesive for all its Babel-like diversity, and a remarkably easy place to get around in.

For those who rate shopping right up there with life's chief imperatives, New York is certainly user-friendly, those numbered streets and avenues gliding you up and down and across Manhattan's asphalt jungle. It's difficult to find a more compelling place than this Cornucopia-on-the-Hudson, sprinkled with assorted boutiques and bodegas, mom-and-pop storefronts, famous department stores, and various well-stocked emporiums and discount outlets all jostling for a piece of the sales action. Prices? They run the gamut from outrageously prohibitive to cheap-cheap. You pays your money and you takes your choice, but the main point is that if you can't find it in Gotham, it doesn't exist.

*Opposite: Downtown bustle at Broadway and Houston. Below: Colorful glassware at Michael Anchin, Brooklyn*

## Spotlight on Manhattan

And when we say Gotham, we're talking Manhattan – East Side, West Side, and all around the town, plus that rather sizable adjunct known as Brooklyn just across the East River. Back in 1898, the city was formally forged from five constituencies – Manhattan, Brooklyn, Queens, the Bronx, and Staten Island – each of the boroughs distinctive in one way or another, the whole metropolitan shebang to be welded together seamlessly by buses, bridges, and subway cars.

Altogether it's one of the world's great shopping centers, and the jewel in the crown is Manhattan. With the exception of the final chapter, which takes a look at Brooklyn's shops and stores, this guide focuses on that slender wedge of land (about 12 miles/19km long and 2 miles/3km wide) tucked in neatly between the East and Hudson rivers. It is of course impossible to include all that Manhattan has to offer, never mind the city as a whole. We'll just try to steer you along the right path and let you take it from there.

## Onward and Upward

In the beginning, Manhattan was all about what we now call downtown, before it began creeping north, from the Seaport up through the Village, then Midtown, the Upper East Side and Upper West Side, Harlem and beyond to the outer boroughs. As for shopping, its history worked somewhat in reverse. There have long been established shopping neighborhoods on both the Upper East and West Sides, while much of southern Manhattan has

traditionally been dominated by business or industry. It's true that downtown neighborhoods such as the West Village and Wall Street have some of the oldest stores and restaurants, but such businesses were created originally to serve their immediate vicinity. Given their history and well-stocked shelves, they have taken these otherwise mundane needs – food and general domestic supplies – and created a market that grows well beyond need.

## Pulling Power

For many years the main inspiration for people to shop in New York was its big department stores – Macy's, Bloomingdale's, Lord & Taylor, Saks Fifth Avenue, to name a few. More recently many have opened branches elsewhere in the US, and this, combined with the fact that the designers whose goods they carry often have their own outlets elsewhere, has meant that the big names have lost some of their luster, though they continue to offer some of the best prices, the best return policies (usually 30 days), and a range of selections that is just not possible in the smaller stores.

Another reason that shoppers have long been drawn to New York is the city's plethora of upmarket boutiques. The designers patronized by movie stars and other celebrities have traditionally been New York-based – Chanel, Oleg Cassini, Emilio Pucci, Diane von Furstenberg, Geoffrey Beene, etc. The desire to look like the people in the magazines, or at least to get a glimpse of where their clothes are made, has brought generations of shoppers to New York. And even if the prices are way beyond your budget, Manhattan has some of the best window shopping in the world.

## Exploring On Foot

New York is a walker's city as well as a shopper's city. It's easily possible to walk around each of the neighborhoods presented in the different chapters of this guide. It also helps that for the most part New York is organized on a straightforward grid plan – numbered streets (north-south) and avenues (east-west). Pay little heed to the fancied-up Avenue of the Americas tag for good old Sixth Avenue, but watch out for the crazy-quilt pattern below 14th Street. In this latter neck of the Manhattan woods, the West Village has streets unique to its neighborhood, many running at odd angles, which makes navigating this area a challenge even for longtime New Yorkers. Things really change south of Houston Street, where the numbers end altogether. Keep in mind that Fifth Avenue and, to the north, Central Park mark the division between east and west.

Some people fear walking around New York because of supposed pickpockets or perhaps would-be murderers, but in fact the city has been experiencing a decline in the rate of crime. Such crime that does occur tends to be as random in nature as anywhere else in the world, and as elsewhere, ostentatious displays of jewelry or wealth tend to invite muggers. Because New York is such a pedestrian-friendly town, and generally a lively place at all hours, there are few locations you should avoid. Most streets are consistently populated – although Midtown and southern Manhattan are more deserted in the evenings, when the East and West Villages are hopping. Central Park and Battery Park are best avoided after dark.

## Subways, Buses, and Taxis

The excellent subway, bus, and taxi systems are a bonus. Subway and bus maps can be obtained from any subway station, whose entrances are easily spotted at street level. Despite reports to the contrary, New York City subways are considered fairly clean and safe – although it's still best to avoid traveling on your own after 10pm. Taxis are easy to become dependent on – unlike most other cities, where you have to arrange for taxis in advance, here they just appear. Fares are reasonable, but if you're trying to get somewhere during the middle of the day or at rush hour, it can be a long, frustrating, and expensive ride. The subway is usually the fastest way of getting around, especially for

*Left: There's always a good bargain to be had in New York. Below: Canal Street vendors.*

long distances, although walking is quicker if you're only traveling a few blocks.

## Selecting Shops

In selecting which shops to include in this guidebook, we wanted to strike a balance between the most popular stores in New York, those that consistently draw rave reviews, and the lesser known up-and-coming shopping neighborhoods and stores. Chain stores can, of course, be found elsewhere in the US and often in other countries, so you needn't prioritize them if time is of the essence. Gap, Banana Republic, The Body Shop, Sephora, Nine West and all the rest are in almost every mall across America; their New York locations, which are several, don't offer any different experience or selections, except perhaps the appeal of visiting a larger store. And next to every one of these is a Starbucks. It's impossible to list all of the chain stores' locations, but most of them are cited or referenced at least once; you'll inevitably run into one as you wander about the neighborhoods covered in this guide.

## From Fashion to Food

Each chapter but the last focuses on a key shopping area of Manhattan and has the same categories of listings – although not every category is covered in every chapter. Fashion is by far the most popular category, simply because most shops in New York fall within this bracket. Health & Beauty stores vary from drugstores of dimestore caliber (mostly Duane Reade) to high-end makeup outlets – and, given this range, are almost as popular as fashion stores. Some of the stores in New York are ridiculously expensive, the most absurd being in furniture, design, and antiques. The number of furniture and design stores listed doesn't reflect the vast array available in New York – but many of these stores are for wealthy connoisseurs or interior designers only, who are sometimes the only ones allowed access. Also, the goods sold are specialty items, and unlikely to be picked up on a day out shopping.

Babies have practically become consumers before they can walk, so there are an increasing number of baby and children's stores, most offering clothes that can't be washed, and bedding that is fit for a queen. These items are more likely to be purchased as gifts rather than by parents, who know how quickly children ruin or grow out of things. And for their mothers, there is now a huge selection of trendy maternity shops. Pregnant women are no longer exempt from New York's tendency to put a premium on fashion.

Food has also been one of New York's most prized possessions, not only in the form of the master chefs and their restaurants but also in the high

## AREA SPECIALTIES AT A GLANCE

**Designer/high-end fashion and accessories**
Soho, Midtown, Upper East Side

**New designers, accessories**
Nolita, Lower East Side, East Village, Brooklyn

**Lingerie**
Nolita

**Re-sale clothing**
East Village

**Shoes**
Soho, Midtown (department stores), Greenwich Village (Eighth Street)

**Bath products, toiletries, make-up**
West Village, Soho

**Department stores**
Midtown, Upper East Side

**Furniture, design, interiors**
Tribeca, Soho, Flatiron District, Brooklyn

**Community bookstores**
Upper East Side, West Village

**Community music stores**
Lower East Side

**Electronics**
Midtown (Fifth and Seventh Avenues), Wall Street (J&R)

**Children's clothing, furniture, toys**
Upper West Side, Upper East Side

**Jewelry & watches**
Midtown

**Souvenirs**
The Seaport, Downtown, Times Square, Canal Street

**Gift shops**
Union Square, Nolita, West Village

**Specialty food shops**
Upper West Side

**Sporting goods**
Union Square

**Antiques**
East Village, Tribeca, Upper East Side

percentage of gourmet markets. Now that you can get Indian spices, kumquat jam and microbrewed beer in markets all across the country, these food shops are less of a novelty, but, desperate to hold onto their niche, they usually stock something that hasn't reached most people's radar; we have included a selection of these. Bookstores and music stores have dwindled in numbers over the past few years. Every New York neighborhood has a story about a Barnes & Noble or a Tower Records or a Circuit City moving in and killing off the friendly community store that was there for decades. In most of the bookstores, coffee shops and comfy couches are a must, so you can linger for hours or make your purchase and move on. Most everything else listed is in the specialty category – cigar shops, garden supplies, and so on.

At the end of each listings section we have included a brief selection of restaurants, bars, and spas to let you unwind from your shopping exertions. Most spa treatments start at around $50, and a tip is expected.

*Left: Michele Varian silky cushions.*
*Below: Flaunt that purchase!*
*Next page: Dean and DeLuca, paradise for gourmets.*

## Shopping Therapy

Shopping inevitably means different things to different people, and New York has done a pretty good job of responding to these varied needs. In general, shopping is both an indulgence and a necessity. For some people it's a release from the rest of our lives, a way to escape our mundane jobs or to add some spice to our lives. Other people are dependent on it as a form of therapy – retail therapy. Making purchases is a way to celebrate a pay raise, mourn a breakup, or attempt to replenish our plummeting self-esteem. For all it's a good excuse to explore new places.

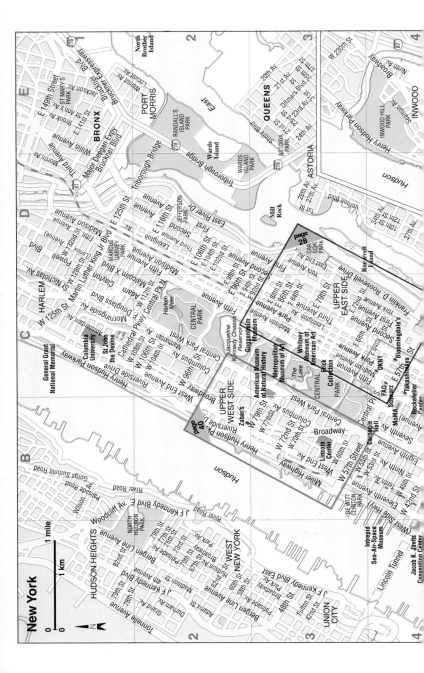

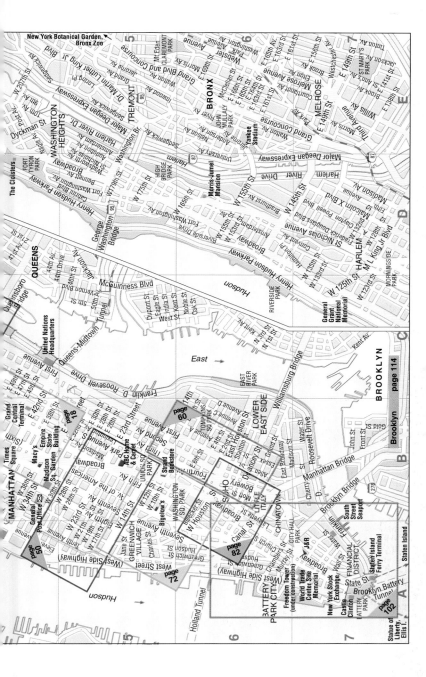

# Area 1: Midtown

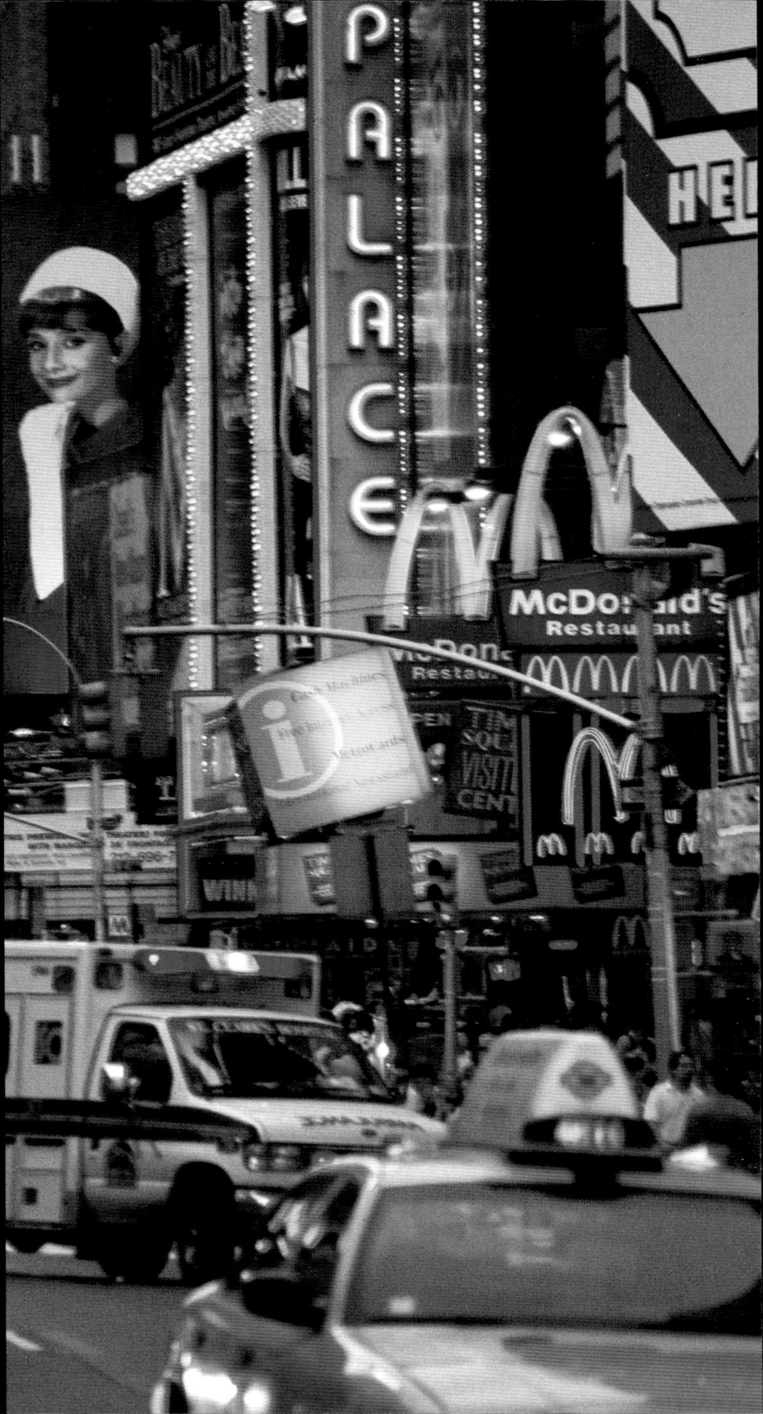

# MIDTOWN

*Smack dab in the middle of the Big Apple it is, and at this central
district's core is a street synonymous with shopping itself – Fifth Avenue*

**M**ost visitors feel they have really arrived in New York when they
confront Midtown Manhattan for the first time. This is not only the
geographical center of the metropolis, but its commercial hub.
Midtown has Fifth Avenue, that most vital artery knifing through the core of
the Big Apple. It has the two big railroad depots, Penn Station and Grand
Central; the busy Port Authority bus terminal close by glitzy Times Square,
still the crossroads of the world; the classically pillared Post Office with its
famous inscription: 'Neither rain nor sleet nor snow nor dark of night...';
brassy 42nd Street and the touristy Rockefeller Center, and the waves of
yellow cabs playing dodge-em with gaggles of pedestrians on streets choked
with traffic. If Manhattan had to settle for just one downtown, this would be
it. Home to stores and all types of commercial enterprise, it's one of the
largest areas of the city, so it has the advantage of having much to choose
from. As well as a full complement of chain stores, Midtown has more
than its fair share of exclusive boutiques and department stores.

*Opposite: The
bright lights of
Times Square.
Below:
Fashion dummy
at Bergdorf
Goodman.*

The main area covered in this chapter is bounded by Sixth Avenue
to the west, Park Avenue to the east, 59th Street (also known as
Central Park South) to the north, and 34th Street to the south. A small
number of stores veer from these suggested boundaries, but the
area of main interest, and the address of the majority of shops
listed, is Fifth Avenue – for many, the very essence of New
York, and for visiting shoppers, invariably the first port of call.

## Fifth Avenue

Fifth Avenue runs through the center of Manhattan Island,
and marks the dividing line between east and west.
Addresses in this part of town are important to note. For
example, 15 East 51st Street and 15 West 51st Street are
within a block of each other. The Midtown stretch of
Fifth Avenue runs from the Empire State Building at
East 34th to Central Park South. Either end would
make a good starting point for your shopping tour.
However, the main concentration of chic shops and department
stores is between Central Park, where you'll find Tiffany's and the
Trump Tower, and Rockefeller Center, which is opposite Saks Fifth
Avenue. Rockefeller Center itself has an underground mall –
nothing special, but it has an impressive food court, and it's a good
place to take cover in bad weather.

Fifth Avenue is home to many of the city's famous department
stores. Apart from Saks, you'll also find the exclusive Bergdorf
Goodman and upscale Henri Bendel and, further down by the Empire
State Building, the more staid Lord & Taylor. A relative newcomer is
the wonderful Japanese department store Takashimaya. Between them,
there is little that these multi-story behemoths don't have to offer.

Fashionable clothing rules on Fifth Avenue, but there's no dearth of jewelry, silver, and gift shops either. Many of the world's top designers have their show-piece stores here – Cartier, Tiffany & Co, Prada, Christian Dior among them.

East of Fifth Avenue and running parallel is Madison Avenue, where smart office workers kit themselves out at Brooks Brothers at 346 Madison on 44th Street. Further east, across Park and Lexington, the historic district of Turtle

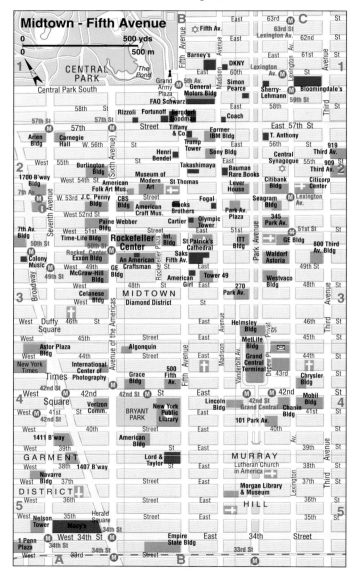

**Midtown - Fifth Avenue**

## LOCAL ATTRACTIONS

The **Rockefeller Center** is a complex of buildings in the heart of Manhattan, with a skating rink, which becomes an outdoor eatery in summer. This is also home to NBC Studios. The week after Thanksgiving, you can go there for the Christmas tree lighting.

Abutting this complex is **St. Patrick's Cathedral**, and a few blocks away are the **American Museum of Folk Art** and **Madame Tussauds Wax Museum,** and the renovated **Museum of Modern Art**. This building itself is a work of art, including the outdoor sculpture garden, a nice retreat on warm days. **Times Square** is west, where you can take in a Broadway show. To the south is **Bryant Park**, which in summer shows outdoor movies; and further south is the **Empire State Building**.

Bay (between 48th and 49th) and swanky Sutton Place (above 54th) are among the classiest addresses in town, with numerous gourmet food shops to match the fancy apartment buildings.

## Lower Midtown

Back on Fifth Avenue, if you venture one block west of the Empire State, at Herald Square, you'll find another New York icon, Macy's. 'The biggest department store in the world' covers a whole block and stocks just about everything money can buy. Just south of Herald Square, the 90 retailers in the Manhattan Mall provide a no-frills, all-American retail experience.

Continue north along Broadway and you'll reach Times Square, transformed in the 1990s from an area of sleaze, crime, and porn to a tourist mecca of hotels, restaurants, and entertainment. Shopping, however, is not one of its strengths. Newly gentrified, but still chaotic, Times Square is the epicenter of the Theater District. This is the place to round off your New York shopping experience with a bite to eat and a Broadway show.

West of Times Square, around Eighth and Ninth Avenues, you'll find Hell's Kitchen and Clinton. Once a notorious slum district (it was the setting for *West Side Story*), it has undergone something of a transformation. Inhabited by a new generation of immigrants, artists, and actors, this is an area of good, cheap, ethnic restaurants and a few stores to match. East of Fifth Avenue, between 34th and 40th, is Murray Hill, a genteel residential district centered around the lovely Morgan Library, but offering little in the way of shopping.

*Macy's grand Broadway entrance.*

*A world of sneakers at Niketown.*

## Fashion & Footwear

### Armani Exchange
*645 Fifth Avenue [B2].*
*Tel: (212) 980-3037.*
*www.armaniexchange.com*
The cheapest of the three tiers of stores in couture designer Giorgio Armani's empire. His mid-priced range is Emporio Armani, while the top end is Giorgio Armani.
BRANCH: 568 Broadway, Soho.

### Brooks Brothers
*666 Fifth Avenue [B2].*
*Tel: (212) 261-9440.*
*www.brooksbrothers.com*
This long-established firm shows a commitment to traditional style while offering updated trends that keep them in the fashion marketplace. There are also lines for women and children.
BRANCHES: across Manhattan.

### Eres
*621 Madison Avenue [B1].*
*Tel: (212) 223-3550.*
*www.eresparis.com*
Eres do women's bathing suits and lingerie, all in bright or pastel colors – and at high prices.
BRANCH: 98 Wooster Street, Soho.

### H&M
*640 Fifth Avenue [B2]. Tel:*
*(212) 489-0390. www.hm.com*
This international Swedish chain does fashionable streetwear at throwaway prices. They also have cosmetics, accessories, lingerie, and a good range of plus sizes.
BRANCHES: across Manhattan.

### Did you know?
Sales are held from mid-December to mid-February and mid-July to mid-August. Department stores tend to offer the best markdowns, with sale items starting at around 30 percent off, with up to 70 percent off by the end of the sale. Holiday weekends – Fourth of July etc. – are also prime times for sales.

### Jay Kos
*475 Park Avenue [C1].*
*Tel: (212) 319-2770.*
*www.jaykos.com*
This store exudes style and class, with its array of beautifully cut shirts and elegant suits made with the finest fabrics. All very New England. Bargain hunters and scruffy urbanites need not apply.

### Niketown
*6 East 57th Street [B2]. Tel:*
*(212) 891-6453. www.nike.com*
This five-floor high-tech store is packed wall-to-wall with products. Name your sport, they'll have a shoe and gear for it.

## Jewelry & Accessories

### Coach
*595 Madison Avenue [B1]. Tel:*
*(212) 754-0041. www.coach.com*
This established brand, known for its quality leather classics, has updated its traditional image in order to compete with accessories guru Kate Spade and other trendy purveyors of bags, purses, and assorted leather goods.
BRANCHES: across Manhattan.
Tel: 888-262-6224 for details.

*Niketown is spread over five levels.*

*Audrey Hepburn,*
*the face of Tiffany.*

### Fortunoff
*3 West 57th Street [B1].*
*Tel: (212) 758-6660.*
*www. fortunoff.com*
Since the 1920s Fortunoff has
been a respected leader in silverware and jewelry. It's not as
fancy as Tiffany & Co., but you
can get better deals here.

### Michael C. Fina
*545 Fifth Avenue [B3].*
*Tel: (212) 557-2500.*
*www.michaelfina.com*
Discounted jewelry, silver, and
china make Fina a favorite among
those registering their bridal lists.

### T. Anthony
*445 Park Avenue [C2]. Tel: (212)*
*750-9797. www.tanthony.com*
This store does canvas and leather
luggage, handbags, photo albums,
and other leather items, in signature bright red and deep purple.

### Tiffany & Co.
*727 Fifth Avenue [B2]. Tel: (212)*
*755-8000. www.tiffany.com*
Tiffany's are in most major
American cities, but this is the shop
made famous by Audrey Hepburn,
in the film *Breakfast at Tiffany's*.
Fabulous silver, jewelry, and china.
BRANCH: 37 Wall Street.

### Tourneau
*12 East 57th Street [B2].*
*Tel: (212) 758-7300.*
*www.tourneau.com*

High-quality watches with a price
to match. There's a large range of
both new and vintage timepieces.
BRANCHES: across Manhattan.

## Health & Beauty

### Crabtree & Evelyn
*520 Madison Avenue [B2].*
*Tel: (212) 758-6419.*
*www.crabtreeevelyn.com*
The floral-scented toiletries and
elegantly packaged teas and cookies look like English imports, but
actually come from Connecticut.
BRANCHES: across Manhattan.
Tel: above number for details.

### Elizabeth Arden
*691 Fifth Avenue [B2].*
*Tel: (212) 546-0200.*
*www.elizabetharden.com*
Stock up on Elizabeth Arden's
make-up and beauty products or
indulge at her Red Door Salon &
Spa (book ahead for massages
and pedicures).

## Department Stores

### Bergdorf Goodman
*754 Fifth Avenue [B1].*
*Tel: (212) 753-7300.*
*www.bergdorfgoodman.com*
The most upmarket and traditional
of New York's department stores,
Bergdorf Goodman has seven

**TIP**
Midtown is as
much a business
destination as it is
a shopping area,
so the quietest
time to shop here
is on the weekend;
bear in mind,
though, that many
of the smaller
stores are closed
on Sundays.

*Macy's is billed as the world's largest department store.*

**TIP**

Department stores usually allow you to return things up to 30 days after your purchase for full credit – and you can usually go over that 30-day limit if you have a good excuse. This goes for sale items, too. Boutiques are much less accommodating – some allow store credit only, no returns on sale items, and no returns or exchanges after seven days. Be aware of these stipulations when making any purchases.

*Glass display at Bergdorf Goodman.*

floors of women's clothes, shoes, jewelry, and health and beauty, and a floor for housewares and children. 'Gentlemen' are catered for in the elegant store across the street.

**Henri Bendel**

*712 Fifth Avenue [B2]. Tel: (212) 247-1100. www.henribendel.com*
Bendel's carries general women's fashion, including sassy designs by Diane von Furstenberg, Rebecca Taylor and Juicy Couture, plus their own line of clothing – mostly inexpensive versions of the designer lines.

**Lord & Taylor**

*424 Fifth Avenue [B5]. Tel: (212) 391-3344. www.lordandtaylor.com*
Lord & Taylor is home to fewer high-end designers than its competitors, focusing instead on more reasonably priced fashions in conservative styles.

**Macy's**

*141 West 34th Street [A5]. Tel: (212) 695-4400. www.macys.com*
Macy's bills itself as the world's largest department store – for some this might be a warning to stay away, while for others it's an invitation to explore. It has a vast array of shoes and clothes, not to mention services including a post office and restaurant. If you happen to be here over Thanksgiving, stay to watch the spectacular parade.

**Saks Fifth Avenue**

*611 Fifth Avenue [B3]. Tel: (212) 753-4000. www.saks.com*
Upmarket Saks is the epitome of the New York department store. It has the greatest range of styles and prices and stocks all the major designers in its make-up, jewelry, luggage, and men's, women's, and children's fashion departments.

**Takashimaya**

*693 Fifth Avenue [B2]. Tel: (800) 753-2038. www.ny-takashimaya.com*
This Japanese department store stands out among its American contemporaries for its elegant, choice merchandise.

# Design & Interiors

### An American Craftsman
*60 West 50th Street [B3].*
*Tel: (212) 307-7161.*
*www.anamericancraftsman.com*
An eclectic collection of hand-made items including furniture, kaleidoscopes, jewelry, and pieces for the home. Many of their products would make memorable gifts.
BRANCH: 790 Seventh Avenue, Midtown.

### American Folk Art Museum
*45 West 53rd Street [B2].*
*Tel: (212) 265-1040.*
*www.folkartmuseum.org*
This museum shop sells replicas of exhibits as well as other items of folk art. It's ideal for those who would love the real thing, but whose budget can't stretch to that.

### MoMA Design Store
*44 West 53rd Street [B2].*
*Tel: (212) 767-1050.*
*www.momastore.org*
The store at the Museum of Modern Art is no ordinary museum gift shop. It sells the usual – postcards, posters, art books, and art-themed novelties, etc. – but there's a range of unique modern furniture and fixtures here too.
BRANCH: 81 Spring Street, Soho.

### Simon Pearce
*500 Park Avenue [C1].*
*Tel: (212) 421-8801.*
*www.simonpearce.com*
Handblown glass, tableware, pottery, and lamps. The designs are elegant without being ostentatious, and the shop, with wooden floors and open air spaces, mirrors the artist's studio in Vermont.

# Books, Music, & Electronics

### Argosy Book Store
*116 East 59th Street [C1].*
*Tel: (212) 753-4455.*
*www.argosybooks.com*
Used, rare, and old books and prints are this store's specialty. For the connoisseur, or for an unusual gift, this shop is a find.

### Bauman Rare Books
*535 Madison Avenue [B2].*
*Tel: (212) 751-0011.*
*www.baumanrarebooks.com*
Bauman's resembles a traditional library of the kind that you might find at an Ivy League college, with a wonderful range of old and rare books.

### Borders
*461 Park Avenue [C2]. Tel: (212) 980-6785. www.bordersstores.com*
This bookstore, part of the vast international chain, is arranged over four floors, and has an excellent music department.
BRANCHES: 550 Second Avenue, Murray Hill; 100 Broadway.

### Colony Music Center
*1619 Broadway [A3]. Tel: (212) 265-2050. www.colonymusic.com*
Comb through Colony's vast sheet music collection, so comprehensive that it has been nominated the World's Largest Karaoke Dealer.

### CompUSA
*420 Fifth Avenue [B5]. Tel: (212) 764-6224. www.compusa.com*
You are guaranteed quality and a warranty on your new computer at CompUSA; it's not the place to come if you like to bargain.
BRANCH: 1775 Broadway

### Rizzoli
*31 West 57th Street [B1].*
*Tel: (212) 759-2424.*
*www.rizzoliusa.com*
This bookseller/publisher knows that its customers often *do* buy a book for its cover – hence their wonderful display of the novels *du jour* and their own beautifully produced art books.

## Children

### American Girl Place
*609 Fifth Avenue [B3].*
*Tel: (877) 247-4223.*
*www.americangirl.com*
More than a store, you can have
your picture taken, take tea, and
see the musical, all with your doll.
A New York institution that draws
girls from around the world to outfit their dolls and even themselves.

### FAO Schwarz
*767 Fifth Avenue [B1]. Tel:*
*(212) 644-9400.www.fao.com*
There is nothing more fun than a
three-story toy store with life-sized
stuffed animals, a baby nursery
filled with dolls, a Barbie runway,
Lego Star Wars characters and
more. A New York institution.

## Food & Drink

### Sherry-Lehmann
*505 Park Avenue [C1].*
*Tel: (212) 838-7500.*
*www.sherry-lehmann.com*
Purveyors of fine wines and spirits
since 1934. The sign offering

delivery to The Hamptons indi-
cates their upmarket clientele, and
the expert staff know their grapes.

## Specialist

### Brookstone
*20 West 57th Street [B2].*
*Tel: (212) 245-1405.*
*www.brookstone.com*
Gadgets are this store's specialty,
from back massagers to ergonomic
gardening tools, and other things
you may be persuaded you need.

### Davidoff
*535 Madison Avenue [B2].*
*Tel: (212) 751-9060.*
*www.davidoff.com*
Cigars, lighters, ashtrays, and
humidors are the focus here. If you
like the smell of cigars – or are a
connoisseur – take a while to
browse here or head down to Nat
Sherman (500 Fifth Avenue).

### Fogal
*515 Madison Avenue [B2]. Tel:*
*(212) 355-3254.www.fogal.com*
Tights that promise not to snag –
and they shouldn't at these prices.
Interesting nylons and bodysuits.

---

### WHERE TO UNWIND

#### Bryant Park Café and Grill
*25 West 40th Street [B4]. Tel: (212) 840-6500*
Attached to the main branch of the New York
City Library, this café and grill has floor-to-
ceiling windows, which give lovely views of
Bryant Park. Good American fare.

#### Frederic Fekkai Beauty Salon
*712 Fifth Avenue [B2]. Tel: (212) 753-9500*
For post-shopping pampering, try this ultra-
deluxe salon in the Bendel building. The spa is
a great treat, but it's popular, so reserve.

#### Carriage Rides
Lined up along Central Park South between
Fifth and Sixth avenues are dozens of horse-

drawn carriages ready to take you for a ride
through Central Park.

#### Mangia
*50 West 57th and 16 East 48th Street [B2/B3]*
*Tel: (212) 582-5882 and Tel: (212) 754-7600*
Upstairs you can sit for breakfast or lunch,
while downstairs offers great take-out.
Prices are discounted after 4pm.

#### The Peninsula Hotel
*700 Fifth Avenue [B2]. Tel: (212) 247-2200*
After a day's shopping, the rooftop bar, Pen
Top, is a great place to have a drink, enjoy the
views, and watch the city move at a much
faster pace below. A well-kept secret.

# The Diamond District

*If you appreciate fine jewelry but can't afford the highest prices, visit 47th Street, where there are bargains to be had*

**A**s you turn onto 47th Street off either Fifth or Sixth Avenues, you are transported into a whole new glittering world. Protected by silver gates at each end, this block is devoted exclusively to jewelry stores, most of which are run by Orthodox Jews. Sporting beards and earlocks, and dressed in their traditional white shirts, black suits, and *yarmulkes,* they mill around the streets, offices, and shop floors doing business with wholesalers, retailers, and shoppers.

This is the diamond district, also known as Diamond Row, and is *the* place to come if you are looking to pick up some jewelry at cost price. It is possible to find the same items sold at Tiffany's and other upmarket outlets at a fraction of the price. Close to $500 million worth of gems are traded in this street every day. Some stores have the appearance of an average jewelry shop with sparkling window displays and storefronts. Others are hidden in office buildings, squeezed together with hundreds of other vendors – most have numbers rather than names.

You should have some knowledge of cuts, settings, quality, and price before attempting to make a purchase – or come here first to have a look, then shop around and compare. These jewelers are aware of what the brand-name jewelry designers are making, and they're conversant in the language of replica – after all, most of the top designers are just borrowing designs they discovered elsewhere. You can take a picture of your favorite designs or a piece of jewelry that you want copied, and with their expert opinion you're likely to be able to order just that.

## Areas of Expertise

Of course, most jewelers have a distinct expertise, working in silver versus gold, for example, on brushed pieces, precious stones, or engagement rings. Most of the experts bill themselves as wholesalers and work principally with dealers. It can therefore be difficult for the average customer to get access to them. Nevertheless, if you are determined, many will be willing to arrange an appointment.

As most of the stores are run by Orthodox or Hasidic Jews who observe the Sabbath, they tend to be closed from before sundown on Friday until Monday morning. So if you're looking for bargain buys in the diamond district, you should plan accordingly.

*On Fifth Avenue and Diamond Row, most of what glistens is gold.*

# BARNEYS NEWYORK

| HOURS | M–F | 10am–8pm |
|---|---|---|
| | Saturday | 10am–7pm |
| | Sunday | 11am–6pm |
| | | |
| FRED'S RESTAURANT | M–F | 11:30am–9pm |
| | Saturday | 10:30am–9pm |
| | Sunday | 10:30am–6pm |
| | (Enter on Madison Avenue) | |

# THE UPPER EAST SIDE

*All the top designers, residents who might have stepped out of fashion magazines, and two old standbys: Barneys and Bloomingdale's*

The best thing that ever happened to Manhattan was carving out a big chunk of open space uptown, calling it Central Park, and thereby preventing a total clogging of the island's arteries. The park neatly separates what some have called the Yuppie West Side and its earnest strivers from the Upper East Side and its leisured class. Silk-Stocking District, the Gold Coast – descriptives like these sum up the Upper East Side, where big concerns are remembering to renew your opera subscription and tipping the doorman at Christmas for walking your poodles, assuming you don't already employ professional dog walkers.

Beginning with the park, there's Fifth Avenue and its renowned mansions and museums. Next over is Madison Avenue, famous for the ad agencies but, more to our point, a shopper's delight with its unbroken stretch of boutiques well stocked with the latest fashion. Then hoity-toity Park Avenue and commercial Lexington Avenue and so on over to the East River. There's much to do, see, and buy in this densely packed neighborhood.

## Doing the Continental

Strolling along Madison may remind you of that last overseas jaunt you took. Most of the designers whose flagship stores line the block are Italian, British, French, or Japanese – Malo, tse, Les Copains, Chloe, Yves St. Laurent, Valentino. And most of their shopping bags or store windows advertise their other locations in Milan, Paris, London, or Tokyo. The majority of these stores have long-established New York branches, and Madison Avenue has been a shopping hub for a long time.

*Opposite: Barneys is one of New York's best known stores. Below: Exclusive men's outfitters.*

On and on they go, this parade of shops with richly mellifluous monikers: Gucci, Baccarat, Lanciani, Issey Miyake, Dolce & Gabbana, Furla, etc., etc. Everything right out of the pages of those glossy fashion mags, in fact. And side by side with the haute couture are all the fixings for an expensive lifestyle – Christofle silver, Pratesi sheets, fur coats, Bang & Olufsen audio equipment. Hermès, Versace, Armani, Calvin Klein, Donna Karan – all have opened stores and set off a competitive chain reaction, each designer outdoing the next not only in terms of clothing design but also in architectural and interior design. Starting at 59th Street and walking up Madison Avenue to 86th Street or thereabouts should sate any shoppers appetite – just walk on and you will find what you are looking for. Some shops are on the numbered streets, mostly 59th, 60th, and 61st, and other avenues, mostly Lexington and Third. But if time is of the essence, stick to Madison and you'll be satisfied, if financially drained.

## A Wide Range

The stores that appear in the listings *(pages 30–34)* are those that tend to be unique to this area, simply worth a visit, or those that offer something that can't be found elsewhere. Fashion is probably the largest commodity on the Upper East Side, but this area is about the most well-rounded of the neighborhoods; it offers a lot of a lot – from fine furnishings to beauty items to specialty food. Upper East is also home to some of the best services in New York – dry cleaning, leather repair, caning, Chinese laundry, tailoring, specialty stationery, home decorating, framing, spectacles. If you're in need of any of these services, just ask around at the local shops.

## Barneys and Bloomie's

The Upper East Side is lucky to count department stores among its residents, and the two in this neighborhood should not be missed. Barneys New York

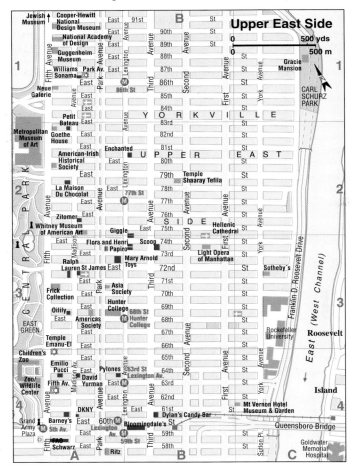

and Bloomingdale's were here long before they opened outlets elsewhere in America. They should be either first or last on your list of shops to visit – first because they give you an overview of everything that awaits you elsewhere in New York, last because once you have decided on what you want to buy, these are often the best shops to patronize. They offer some of the best prices and the best return policies – although this doesn't mean that they necessarily have the most comprehensive collections. Barneys and Bloomingdale's, like most other New York department stores, essentially take everything you see on Madison Avenue and elsewhere in New York and put it under one roof.

## LOCAL ATTRACTIONS

When you have tired of the shops, a stroll through the open spaces of **Central Park** is a great respite – even if you have to dodge the roller-bladers, bikers, and runners at weekends. In warm weather, it's fun to see the roller-bladers discoing around a circle off the 72nd Street cut-through. In the park, you can rent bikes or rowboats from The Boathouse, which is just north of the 72nd Street cut-through, or just sit and sip iced tea at The Boathouse restaurant.

Fifth Avenue is also known as museum mile. The **Frick Collection**, the **Jewish Museum**, the **Guggenheim Museum**, **Cooper Hewitt**, and the **Metropolitan Museum of Art**, among others, can be found along this famous thoroughfare. Each has a gift shop for museum replications and other arts and craft items.

Each houses mini-boutiques for items by top designers; Barneys carries fewer commercial designers, like Paul Smith and Jill Sander, and Bloomingdale's has individual sections for more casual lines, like Theory and Tommy Hilfiger. Both have their own brand of clothing, which is often some of the least expensive in the store. Both also have excellent home furnishing departments; Bloomingdale's has an entire floor devoted to furniture. Luggage, handbags, lingerie, and perfumes can all be found, too. The makeup sections have counters devoted to most brand-name cosmetics, and they offer free makeovers – with the hope that you'll buy some of the products sampled. Barneys also takes on a few products by emerging designers, so you can often find one-of-a-kind stuff tucked in here.

*Upper East Side apartments alongside Central Park.*

*Zitomer (see page 32) stocks a huge range of bath and beauty products.*

## Fashion & Footwear

### Arche
*995 Madison Avenue [A2]. Tel: (212) 439-0700.*
Unadventurous, but the soft leather and spongy soles make these French shoes the best for casual comfort.
BRANCHES: across Manhattan.

### Betsey, Bunky, Nini
*980 Lexington Avenue [A3]. Tel: (212) 744-6716.*
Founded by three friends, this small boutique carries all the sophisticated urban designers you'd find in a department store, minus the crowds.

### DKNY
*655 Madison Avenue [A4]. Tel: (212) 223-3569. www.dkny.com*
Donna Karan's casual line. The high-end boutique is uptown *(see below)*. Urban chic at its best.
BRANCH: 420 West Broadway, Soho. **Donna Karan**, 819 Madison Avenue, Upper East Side.

### Emilio Pucci
*24 East 64th Street [A4]. Tel: (212) 752-4777. www.emiliopucci.com*
The 1960s master of psychedelic designs and bold graphic prints has made a big comeback.
BRANCH: 701 Fifth Avenue, Midtown

### Liz Lange Maternity
*958 Madison Avenue [A2]. Tel: (212) 879-2191.*

*Step into the 60s in a Pucci store, this is the 5th Avenue branch.*

*www.lizlange.com*
Fashionable clothing for women who refuse to go through their pregnancy looking frumpy.

### Oilily
*820 Madison Avenue [A3]. Tel: (212) 772-8686. www.oilily-world.com*
Featuring women's and children's clothes, this store, with its bright, wildly designed clothing, brings out the child in all of us. In a city specializing in black, these reds, pinks, blues, and oranges stand out.
BRANCH: 465 West Broadway,

### Polo Ralph Lauren
*867 Madison Avenue [A3]. Tel: (212) 606-2100. www.ralphlauren.com*
Housed in the "Polo Mansion," this store covers the entire collection of Ralph Lauren's clean-cut Ivy League fashions for men and women. Blazers, tweed jackets, cable-knit sweaters, and evening wear, plus shoes, accessories, and household linens. Children's and sports wear are across the street.

### R.M. Williams
*46 East 59th Street [A4]. Tel: (212) 308-1808. www.rmwilliams.com*
The Australian designer's store features oilskin coats, leather boots, and other rugged clothing worn down under.

## Roberta Freymann
*153 East 70th Street [B3].*
*Tel: (212) 585-3767.*
*www.roberta-freymann.com*
Resort wear for your next trip to a sunny, luxurious location: cotton tunics and bright colors. The branch location has a cute line for children as well as housewares.
BRANCH: Roberta Roller Rabbit, 1019 Lexington Avenue.

## Scoop
*1275 Third Avenue [B3].*
*Tel: (212) 535-5577.*
*www.scoopnyc.com*
Scoop offers up-to-the-minute urban chic displayed by color rather than designer label. For sale items, head for the 'Scoop It Up' section.
BRANCH: across Manhattan.

## Searle
*1124 Madison Avenue [A1].*
*Tel: (212) 988-7318.*
*www.searlenyc.com*
Most famous for their shearling coats and trendy outerwear, this well-stocked branch also has a good collection of stylish ready-to-wear, shoes, and accessories.
BRANCHES: across Manhattan.

## Unisa
*701 Madison Avenue [A4]. Tel: (212) 753-7474. www.unisa.com*

The most reasonably priced ladies' shoes on the Upper East Side, with a variety of fashionable casual, and practical footwear.

# Jewelry & Accessories

## David Yurman
*729 Madison Avenue [A4].*
*Tel: (212) 752-4255.*
*www.davidyurman.com*
Yurman's distinctive gold and silver jewelry is regularly featured in fashion magazines; this is the place to check out his entire line.

## Georg Jensen
*685 Madison Avenue [A4].*
*Tel: (212) 759-6457.*
*www.georgjensen.com*
The distinctive pounded and delicately woven silverware and silver jewelry of the eponymous Danish design school are on sale here, as well as watches and other items.

## Julie Artisans' Gallery
*762 Madison Avenue [A4].*
*Tel: (212) 717-5959.*
*www.julieartisans.com*
Handcrafted jewelry and clothing made by different artisans, so striking it won't go unnoticed.

## Longchamp
*713 Madison Avenue [A4].*
*Tel: (212) 223-1500.*
*www.longchamp.com*
This French bag company has made a nice home for itself in New York. Its handbags and other leather goods are well made, practical, and chic.
BRANCH: 132 Spring Street.

# Health & Beauty

## Clyde's
*926 Madison Avenue [A3].*
*Tel: (212) 744-5050.*
*www.clydesonline.com*
An Aladdin's cave of health and beauty products that does a roar-

**TIP**

If you like gyms, the Equinox fitness center is a great one, and if you arrange for a spa service – manicure, waxing, haircut – at The Spa at Equinox, you get full access to the gym, so you can make a morning of it. There is a great pool, steam room, yoga classes and all fitness equipment. Plus, there's a great shop on the main floor, in case you left your workout clothes at home. Equinox is located at the corner of East 63rd Street and Lexington, tel: (212) 750 4900.

*Left: Watches at*
*Georg Jensen.*

ing trade, despite the popularity of its more established neighbor, Zitomer's *(see below)*. There is also an in-store pharmacy.

### Zitomer

*969 Madison Avenue [A2].*
*Tel: (212) 737-5560.*
*www.zitomer.com*
Three storys packed with every bath and beauty product imaginable. Also stocks children's toys and an overwhelming choice of fun and functional hair accessories.
BRANCH: Z Chemists, 40 West 57th Street.

## Department Stores

### Barneys New York

*660 Madison Avenue [A4].*
*Tel: (212) 826-8900.*
*www.barneys.com*
The department store for style slaves of all ages, where you can blow a fortune on the latest lines of top designers from the trad to the trendy. Famous for its warehouse sales held in their Chelsea store.
BRANCHES: 236 West 18th Street, Chelsea; 116 Wooster Street, Soho.

### Bloomingdale's

*1000 Third Avenue [B4].*
*Tel: (212) 705-2000.*
*www.bloomingdales.com*
This New York institution is the epitome of a department store. An entire block full of clothing, toys, household goods, luggage, and china. Top designers – Marc Jacobs, Calvin Klein, Donna Karan, Armani – have mini-boutiques here, as do more moderately priced Tahari, Theory, and BCBG.
BRANCH: 504 Broadway, Soho.

## Design & Interiors

### Adrien Linford

*927 Madison Avenue [A3].*
*Tel: (212) 628-4500.*
When you want to find something original for your home or yourself this is the place to come; stylish salt-and-pepper shakers, unusual bookends, necklaces and handbags.
BRANCH: 1339 Madison Avenue, Upper East Side.

### Crate & Barrel

*650 Madison Avenue [A4].*
*Tel: (212) 308-0011.*

**TIP**

Twice a year – late August to early September, and mid-to-late February – there is the famous Barneys Sale at the Chelsea store. You can usually get good buys; late in the sale items can be 70 percent off the initial heavily discounted price, but be prepared for chaos!

*Bloomingdale's is a New York landmark.*

*www.crateandbarrel.com*
Famous as a mail order catalogue long before it had a presence in New York, Crate & Barrel caters to all your household needs from margarita glasses to measuring cups. Very good for wedding gifts.
BRANCH: 611 Broadway, Soho.

**Gracious Home**
*1220 Third Avenue [B3].*
*Tel: (212) 517-6300.*
*www.gracioushome.com*
Be it a lamp, shower curtain, bed sheets, or hammer you're after, this hardware store carries every household accessory. Departments that specialize in lighting, bedroom, bathroom, and hardware.
BRANCHES: across Manhattan.

**La Terrine**
*1024 Lexington Avenue [A3].*
*Tel: (212) 988-3366.*
*www.laterrinedirect.com*
French pastel and Italian warm-hued dishes, plates, mugs, and entertaining accoutrements are crammed into this small store, which has been here for decades.

**The Metropolitan Museum of Art Store**
*1000 Fifth Avenue [A2].*
*Tel: (212) 570-3894.*
*www.metmuseum.org/store*
The popularity of the posters, replica jewelry and note cards here means there are branches across the world. Stopping by the original store is worth the experience.
BRANCHES: across New York City.

**Sara**
*950 Lexington Avenue [B3].*
*Tel: (212) 772-3243.*
*www.saranyc.com*
Asian-influenced tableware, much of which is almost too pretty or delicate for actual use.

**Williams Sonoma**
*1175 Madison Avenue [A1].*
*Tel: (212) 289-6832.*
*www.williams-sonoma.com*
Williams Sonoma has all you need and more for the perfectly kitted-out kitchen.
BRANCHES: across Manhattan.

**William Wayne & Company**
*850 Lexington Avenue [B4].*
*Tel: (212) 288-9243.*
*www.william-wayne.com*
Full of eccentric little finds – monkey-shaped candelabras, cocktail napkins, fancy footstools.
BRANCHES: 40 University Place, Greenwich Village.

# Books, Gifts, & Souvenirs

**The Corner Bookstore**
*1313 Madison Aveune [off map]. Tel: (212) 831-3554.*
A mainstay on the upper east side, this small bookstore has survived the onslaught of chains with satisfied readers who want their store clerks opinion about what to read.

**E.A.T. Gifts**
*1062 Madison Avenue [A2].*
*Tel: (212) 861-2544.*
*www.elizabar.com/eat*
E.A.T. Gifts is a store for the child in each of us. Its cute candy necklaces and frivolous gifts prove that excess can be fun.

**Pylones**
*842 Lexington Avenue [A4].*
*Tel: (212) 317-9822.*
*www.pylones-usa.com*
Everything from maracas to toasters to hairbrushes to clocks. The one common feature is that they are all brightly colored and playful. Great for gifts–to give and to get.

# Children

**Enchanted**
*1179 Lexington Avenue [B2].*
*Tel: (212) 288-3383*
Walking in this store is like enter-

ing a tree house. It is filled with European toy makers with wooden toys mainly for younger children and there is incentive to shop: the proceeds are used to underwrite scholarships for a nearby school.

**Flora and Henri**
*1023 Lexington Avenue [B2].*
*Tel: (212) 249-1695.*
*www.florahenri.com*
Children's clothing that you might wish came in adult sizes. Soft cottons and flannels, and other basic fabrics to match the simple styles and natural color schemes.

**Giggle**
*1033 Lexington Avenue [B2/3].*
*Tel: (212) 249-4249.*
*www.giggle.com*
Catering mostly to parents of younger children, there is a great display of furniture, and strollers. There is a selection of infant and toddler clothing and most things a child needs for their first years.

**Mary Arnold Toys**
*1010 Lexington Avenue [A3].*
*Tel: (212) 744-8510.*
If you don't want to tackle FAO Schwartz, come to this toy store, which has an equal range of carefully selected toys minus the chaos. Here you also find personal service and knowledgeable sales clerks.

**Petit Bateau**
*1094 Madison Avenue [A2].*
*Tel: (212) 988-8884.*

*www.petit-bateau.com*
Really a children's shop, but their T-shirts are popular with women. In France they sell for about $8; here they mark them up 100 percent, though they are still a good deal and come in great colors.

# Food & Drink

**Dylan's Candy Bar**
*1011 Third Avenue [B4].*
*Tel: (646) 735-0078.*
*www.dylanscandybar.com*
Hyper stimulation at this "sweet" emporium. While her father tackles fashion, Dylan Lauren is taking on the world of candy. All your favorites from childhood and new creations galore.

**La Maison Du Chocolat**
*1018 Madison Avenue [A2].*
*Tel: (212) 744-7117.*
*www.lamaisonduchocolat.com*
This chocolate looks too good to eat. You can splurge here, but if it's too intimidating, there are Godiva chocolaterias everywhere.
BRANCH: Rockefeller Center.

# Specialist

**Il Papiro**
*1021 Lexington Avenue [B3].*
*Tel: (212) 288-9330.*
Buying marbleized Italian paper from the source ensures that you get excellent quality as well as a great selection.

**Papyrus**
*1270 Third Avenue [B3].*
*Tel: (212) 717-1060.*
*www.papyrusonline.com*
When Kate's Paperie *(see page 89)* moved in next door, it seemed that Papyrus would be put out of business. But their birthday cards, wrapping papers, and Crane's stationery have kept on selling.
BRANCHES: across Manhattan.

*The Guggenheim is one of the world's great museums.*

*EAT Cafe for a superior sandwich.*

## WHERE TO UNWIND

### Candle Cafe
*1307 Third Avenue [B2]*
*Tel: (212) 472-0970*
Macrobiotic food so flavorful that you may forget it's healthy. Fresh juices, greens, and beans of the day, and desserts without the usual fats and artificial sweeteners. They also have a full-service, more elegant restaurant up the street, Candle 79.

### The Carlyle Hotel
*35 East 76th Street [A2]*
*Tel: (212) 744-1600*
Reservations are recommended if you want to catch Woody Allen, Barbara Cook or other lounge singers who frequent the Cafe Carlyle. There is a hefty cover charge if music is playing, but it might not be obvious, so make sure to inquire. The hotel restaurant also serves a great Sunday brunch. Kids can come, too, and enjoy the Madeline's Tea in Bemelman's Bar.

### E.A.T Cafe
*1064 Madison Avenue [A2]*
*Tel: (212) 772-0022*
Wonderful salads and sandwiches, take-out and eat-in; expensive, but worth it.

### Metropolitan Museum of Art
*1000 Fifth Avenue [A2]*
*Tel: (212) 879-5500*
Friday and Saturday evenings in summer, the rooftop sculpture garden here often has live jazz. A great place to sip champagne and take in the Manhattan skyline. The museum is closed on Monday and some holidays.

### Sarabeths@The Whitney Museum
*945 Madison Avenue [A2]*
*Tel: (212) 570-3670*
Sarabeths has other restaurant locations in New York City, but this one also gets you free entry into the Whitney Museum. If you tell the ticket takers that you are going to the restaurant, you don't have to pay the museum's hefty admission fee. This is a great breakfast or lunch spot – pumpkin muffins, velvety cream of tomato soup and four flowers juice are some of their specialties. The museum is closed on Monday and some holidays.

# Wedding Dresses

*Marriages may be made in heaven, but some of the best wedding dresses are made in New York*

**A**ll roads lead to New York for prospective brides and their proud moms in the market for wedding dresses. The city is well stocked with shops large and small offering them. And there's an infinite number of places equipped with all the paraphernalia needed for that special day – from brides-maids dresses and tuxedos to shoes, veils, rings and, of course, wedding gifts.

Given that there are so many other posh boutiques on the Upper East Side, it's no surprise that this is the best area to find that exquisite wedding dress. The most famous designer has to be Vera Wang, whose dresses start at $3,000, not including alterations, and easily go beyond the $10,000 mark. Nearby are Yumi Katsura, Michelle Roth, and Jane Wilson Marquis, all matching the individuality of Wang's designs, while offering slightly better prices. And all stock shoes, bags, scarves, veils, and other accessories to match. The department stores, notably Bergdorfs and Saks, also have fulsome inventories and carry a range of designer gowns. It might be best to start at one of these stores to get a sense of what's out there, and acquaint yourself with the endless possibilities: assistants at the big stores tend to be more helpful to beginners.

For the bravest of the would-be brides, New York has wedding dress sample sales, which often requires getting up at the crack of dawn to slug it out with others over the discounted gowns. *New York Magazine* lists these sales, and the designers themselves may be willing to share this information with you. And though it's a far cry from the Upper East Side, deep into Brooklyn is Kleinfelds, which offers most brand-named designer dresses at a discount. All these stores require an appointment, so call before visiting; they'll all quickly remind you that these dresses take months to make, so you order early enough.

## Something Different

If you're hoping to be a less conventional bride, or simply can't fathom spending thousands of dollars on a wedding dress, New York has lots to offer here too. There are a few designers and unconventional boutiques in the East Village and Soho – Blue, Morgane LeFay, Legacy – who'll work with you to create

*Wedding party limos, New York style.*

your own individual design, or offer one of their less traditional creations. In addition, most of the top designers offer something long and white. Most of the wedding dress shops also sell dresses for bridesmaids, or have neighboring stores that do. Other favorites are Nicole Miller and Thread.

For shoes, Peter Fox and Stuart Weitzman are the places to go – they can dye shoes or recommend a dyer if you're seeking a perfect match for your dress or the bridesmaids' dresses.

*A sumptuous Vera Wang creation.*

## Wedding Gifts

There's no end to the places where you can register for gifts. Most of the national chain and catalogue companies, such as Crate & Barrel, Williams Sonoma, Pottery Barn, Tiffany's and Michael C. Fina, have New York locations. There's also The Knot website (www. theknot.com), which offers an array of desirable gifts, and most of the department stores and specialty linen, china, and silver shops all offer bridal registry.

## USEFUL ADDRESSES

- **Vera Wang**, 991 Madison Avenue, tel: (212) 628-3400.
- **Jane Wilson Marquis**, 42 East 76th Street, tel: (212) 452-5335.
- **Designer Loft**, 226 West 37th Street, #1501, (Midtown), tel: (212) 944-9013.
- **Legacy**, 109 Thompson Street (Soho), tel: (212) 966-4827.
- **Blue**, 137 Avenue A (East Village), tel: (212) 228-7744.
- **Stuart Weitzman**, 625 Madison Avenue (Midtown), tel: (212) 750-2555.
- **Nicole Miller**, 780 Madison Avenue, tel: (212) 288-9779.
    Also at 77 Greene Street (Soho), tel: (212) 219-1825.
- **Thread**, 26 West 17th Street (Chelsea), tel: (212) 414-8844.
- **Selia Yang**, 71 Franklin Street, (Tribeca), tel: (212) 941-9073.
- **Morgane Le Fay**, 746 Madison Avenue, tel: (212) 879 9700.
    Also at 67 Wooster Street (Soho), tel: (212) 219-7672.
- **Kleinfeld's Bridal**, 110 West 20th Street (Union Square), tel: (646) 633- 4320.

## Gifts

**Crate & Barrel** *(see page 32)*; **The Knot** (www.theknot.com, tel: 877 843 5668); **Michael C. Fina** *(see page 21)*; **Pottery Barn** *(see page 45)*; **Tiffany's** *(see page 21)*; **Williams Sonoma** *(see page 33)*.

NB: The above are Upper East Side addresses unless otherwise indicated.

# THE UPPER WEST SIDE

*For well-known stores, gourmet foods and the sense that you have stepped into a Woody Allen film, this is the place to be*

It's certainly not the only neighborhood in New York City to harbor chain stores, but the Upper West Side has more than its share. In fact it is a common misconception that these are the only stores to be found here. Au contraire. The neighborhood has two main shopping staples – chain stores and long-time family businesses.

This was a New York residential neighborhood before most others, and while it continues to cater to traditional patrons through such homegrown businesses as Zabars, Harry's Shoes and Morris Bros, it seeks to satisfy the shopping whims of the younger crowd via trendy clothing stores such as Gap, Banana Republic, and Betsey Johnson. Some of the chains are unique to New York, but most are national in scope and found all across America. So they're likely to be familiar to anyone visiting the city from other parts.

These well-known labels are almost shorthand for American lifestyles – and are frequently cited as an example of US-led globalization and consumption at the expense of others. This perspective is important only to the extent that some people snarl at such stores, while others are dependent on them either for reasonably priced goods or for a need to 'fit in'. The only icon of Americana that may be more common across the country than these chain stores is McDonald's – or Starbucks, of which there must be a dozen or so on the Upper West Side alone.

*Opposite: Allan & Suzi specializes in vintage chic.*

While some locals are disturbed to see their once distinctive neighborhood take on the look of an outdoor mall, others welcome it as a sign of keeping up with changing times and simplifying their lives. The Upper West Side still has a community feel and likes to think of itself as family-friendly. People here don't wear suits to Sunday brunch; in fact, they're more likely to look like Gap mannequins – the stores come to life.

*Below: Educational rulers at Penny Whistle Toys.*

## Major Arteries

There are three major roads of special interest traversing the Upper West Side: Broadway, Columbus Avenue, and Amsterdam Avenue. The first needs no introduction. A world-class street, Broadway is unique in running the entire length of Manhattan. It starts way downtown, at the Customs House in the financial district, and sweeps diagonally through almost every neighborhood covered in this guide, plus many others, until it comes to an end where the Bronx begins. If you've got the time, hop aboard a Broadway bus running along its full length for a brief tour of Manhattan's varied neighborhoods. Broadway is a strictly commercial thoroughfare that sums up the melting pot that is New York City. There's no block in its headlong rush through the Big Apple that doesn't have one store or another, from Dominican bodegas to pet

stores, Urban Outfitters, and the ubiquitous Duane Reade drugstores. Broadway sums up the city's broad range, from discount to ultra-expensive, local to international.

Columbus Avenue and Amsterdam Avenue both run parallel to Broadway. They've become, late in life, pretty much indistinguishable from each other in their range of stores. The listings in this chapter include a wide selection from each avenue. The Upper West Side's other avenues and most of its side streets are residential in character.

This guide's terminal point is 96th Street, although technically the Upper West Side runs past 110th Street. The designation Upper West Side is really determined by Central Park, on the opposite side of which is Upper East. Harlem is at the northern end, while the southern edge rubs up against the start of Midtown (at Columbus Circle). There are stores in the northern stretch as well, many catering to the Columbia University community (on Morningside Heights).

## A Ready-made Set

Woody Allen, though he himself has moved on up to the East Side, is emblematic of the Upper West Side mind-set, most particularly its modern-day Jewish flavor. He pokes his shtick with Wildean flair at the neurotic New Yorker who

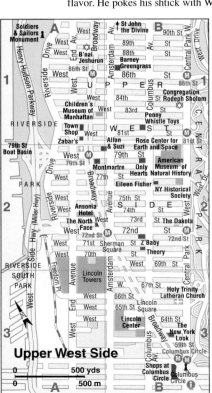

Upper West Side

sees a therapist daily, sends his kids to Hebrew school before they can walk, and has intense friends who end up doing more harm than good. Much stereotyping, much fun. Allen fans new to the neighborhood might feel like they've stepped right onto a movie set. There are lots of familiar sights, too, for those keen on Nora Ephron's films *(Heartburn, You've Got Mail)*. This is a picturesque part of a wonderful town, close to what people conjure up when they visualize New York – brownstones with kids sitting on the stoop, Central Park, traffic and parking nightmares, *Seinfeld*, *Sex and the City*, hot dog vendors, and the Dakota apartment block where John Lennon and others of note once lived. It all makes for great wandering around – just keep out of the way of all the baby-strollers that seem to exist here in disproportionate numbers. The shopping may not be what lures you here, but the neighborhood's history probably will.

## The Joy of Food

Actually, what brings so many people to the Upper West Side – apart, that is, from its dominant attraction, the Lincoln Center for the Performing Arts

– is the food. Some flock to H&H Bagels – over 60,000 freshly baked on the premises every day. Others in the know patronize Barney Greengrass – as much a store as a restaurant, with some of the best smoked fish around. In fact, Barney is second only to Murray's Sturgeon Shop around the corner. Fairway is more than your standard market, and if you happen to make it up to their warehouse on 127th Street, you'll find everything you need. For a long time, Citarella's specialty was fish, but it has grown into a full-scale gourmet market.

There are lots of other food stores on the Upper West Side, as well as elsewhere in the city; we've singled out quality places that people go out of their way to visit. And this is not always easy for New Yorkers who have to hail a cab or take the subway to bring the stuff home. It's common to see lines extending out the door at most of these places, especially around the holidays. If you're in charge of bringing the caviar or pie to the Thanksgiving dinner, plan well ahead.

There's an especially lively restaurant-plus-boutique ambience on Columbus Avenue that attracts twenty-, thirty- and forty-somethings, mostly in the evening hours, and Amsterdam Avenue has also come to life in this regard. The food offerings are grandly diverse and multicultural, and the shop scene is similarly variegated.

## LOCAL ATTRACTIONS

Before **The Dakota** was known as the place where John Lennon was shot, it was famous as one of the first apartment buildings (it dates from 1884) in New York City. Today it attracts tourists for both reasons, but high security means you can only peek into the courtyard and admire from the street. Next to the Dakota is the section of **Central Park** known as Strawberry Fields, which includes a mosaic tribute to Lennon's song, *Imagine*. And while the Upper East Side is known for its Museum Mile, the Upper West Side has a number of museums to choose from, too, including the **Museum of Natural History**, the **New York Historical Society**, and the **Children's Museum of Manhattan**, plus other cultural symbols such as **St John the Divine** and **Lincoln Center**, (under renovation until 2009) home to the Metropolitan Opera and the New York City Ballet.

*Lincoln Center.*

## Fashion & Footwear

### Allan & Suzi
*416 Amsterdam Avenue [A2].
Tel: (212) 724-7445.
www.allanandsuzi.net*
High-end vintage and second-hand
clothing, from 1930s couture
gowns and 1950s prom dresses to
Gaultier, Westwood, Versace, and
other discounted designer seconds.

### Banana Republic
*2360 Broadway [A1].
Tel: (212) 787-2064.
www.bananarepublic.com*
Popular high-street chain with
reasonably priced, conservatively
chic clothing for men and women
– washable cottons and linens and
solid-color suits and trousers. Also
shoes and accessories.
BRANCHES: across Manhattan.
Tel: 888-277-8953 for details.

### Betsey Johnson
*248 Columbus Avenue [B2].
Tel: (212) 362-3364.
www.betseyjohnson.com*
Betsey Johnson makes clothes
with attitude – brightly colored
animal prints, rhinestone-trimmed
sweaters and outrageously sexy
dresses for the wild at heart. The
Soho store has a larger selection
of formal wear.
BRANCHES: 251 East 60th Street,

Upper East Side; 1060 Madison
Avenue, Upper East Side; 138
Wooster Street, Soho.

### Club Monaco
*2376 Broadway [A1]. Tel: (212)
579-2587. www.clubmonaco.com*
Style- and price-wise, Club
Monaco and Banana Republic are
very much in the same vein, but
while Banana Republic sticks
more closely to the practical and
classic, Club Monaco takes the
same fashions and gives them a
more contemporary twist. Good
wardrobe staples at fair prices.
BRANCHES: across Manhattan.
Tel: above number for details.

### Eileen Fisher
*341 Columbus Avenue [B2].
Tel: (212) 362-3000.
www.eileenfisher.com*
Comfort and easy care are the
main priorities of this designer,
with women's separates in soft
cottons and linens of many hues.
BRANCHES: across Manhattan.
Tel. (800) 345 3362 for details.

### Filene's Basement
*2222 Broadway [A2].
Tel: (212) 873-8000.
www.filenesbasement.com*
Not the place to come if you're
short on time as there are stacks of
marked down designer and department store brands to wade through,
but if you've plenty of staying
power then you're sure to find some
real bargains. The shoe department
is definitely worth a look.
BRANCHES: 620 Sixth Avenue,
Chelsea; 4 Union Square, Flatiron.

### Gap
*67th and Broadway [B3]. Tel:
(212) 721-5304. www.gap.com*
The global clothes chain needs
no introduction. Few people are
unfamiliar with the easy-wear
casual khaki, cotton, and denim
styles. At this location you can
take in the whole Gap family,

*Discounted
designer wares
at Allan & Suzi.*

*Only Hearts: gift items and hearts galore.*

including Gap Kids and Baby Gap. All clothes are reasonably priced, and the permanent sale rack usually has some great finds. BRANCHES: across Manhattan. Tel 800-427-7895 for details.

## Harry's Shoes
*2299 Broadway [A1]. Tel: (212) 874-2035. www.harrys-shoes.com*
For decades this shoe shop has been a favorite for families on the Upper West Side, and it has enough of a variety of brands and styles to outfit the entire family.

## Montmartre
*2212 Broadway [A2].*
*Tel: (212) 875-8430.*
*www.montmartreny.com*
Whether you're looking for something to wear to the office, a cocktail party or a picnic in the park, this store has a good assortment of women's clothing from the casual to the chic. An Upper West Side mainstay.

## The New York Look
*30 Lincoln Plaza, Broadway & 62nd Street [B3].*
*Tel: (212) 765-4758.*
Several locations throughout Manhattan, each carrying the same ladies' fashion lines, as well as shoes, handbags, and jewelry, by a variety of designers and in a range of prices. The name says it all.

BRANCHES: across Manhattan. Tel: above number for details.

## The North Face
*2101 Broadway [A2].*
*Tel: (212) 362-1000.*
*www.thenorthface.com*
This clothing store is a beacon for gear-heads and other adventurers. Great selection of camping and hiking equipment.

## Olive & Bette's
*252 Columbus Avenue [B2].*
*Tel: (212) 579-2178.*
*www.oliveandbettes.com*
Trendy women's clothes at reasonable prices. T-shirts by Free People and Autumn Cashmere sweaters, and other hip streetwear. More downtown than uptown. BRANCHES: 1070 Madison Avenue, Upper East Side; 158 Spring Street, Soho; 384 Bleecker Street, West Village.

## Only Hearts
*386 Columbus Avenue [B2].*
*Tel: (212) 724-5608.*
*www.onlyhearts.com*
Only Hearts has its own line of sexy ladies' lingerie and nightwear, but also carries lingerie by other designers such as Capucine and Cosabella. They also stock bags, bath oils, jewelry, and other gift items all of which are either heart-shaped, packaged in a heart

**TIP**

Finally New York has a fancy shopping mall in the center of it all: Time Warner Center, 10 Columbus Circle. Tel: (212) 823-6300. Home to some of New York's best restaurants and dozens of high-end stores – everything from stereo equipment at Bose to make-up at Sephora and clothing at J. Crew.

shape, or printed with hearts. This branch is packed with stuff; the Nolita location is more spacious but has a smaller selection.
BRANCH: 230 Mott Street, Nolita.

### Patagonia
*426 Columbus Avenue [B1]. Tel: (917) 441-0011. www.patagonia.com*
When you are headed to the great outdoors, head first to Patagonia. They can outfit you in Gortex jackets, fleece pants, and thermal underwear to keep you warm.
BRANCH: 101 Wooster Street, Soho.

### Really Great Things
*300 Columbus Avenue [B2]. Tel: (212) 787-5354.*
This store carries fabulous women's fashion – clothing, bags, jewelry, and shoes; also unique items from brand-name designers.
BRANCH: 1048 Third Avenue.

### Sean
*224 Columbus Avenue [B2]. Tel: (212) 769-1489.*
A menswear collection for those who want something different from the usual khakis and collared shirts, but are not ready for the hipness factor of Barneys or Prada.
BRANCH: 132 Thompson Street.

### Theory
*230 Columbus Avenue [B2]. Tel: (212) 362-3676. www.theory.com*
Always on the cutting edge of fashion, Theory does very moderately priced women's casual and business attire.
BRANCH: 151 Spring Street.

### Town Shop
*2273 Broadway [A1]. Tel: (212) 724-8160. www.townshop.com*
This is an old-school lingerie shop, where the shop assistants know your bra size just by looking. Though the store clerks don't seem to have changed in 50 years, the shop does manage to keep up with the times, and the wide selection should be able to satisfy any age or personal preference.

### Variazioni
*2389 Broadway [A1]. Tel: (212) 595-1760.*
Like Intermix *(see p52)* this store has a variety of designers and a focus on carrying styles that come and go with the seasons. Its own designer lines are marginally cheaper than those at Intermix.
BRANCH: 23 Prince Street, Soho.

## Health & Beauty

### The Body Shop
*2159 Broadway [A2]. Tel: (212) 721-2947. www.bodyshop.com*

**TIP**
The Hayden Planetarium is one of the Museum of Natural History's latest additions; on Friday nights it stays open late offering tapas, drinks, and live music. The museum also has a great gift store that is extremely child-friendly.

*Recharging batteries on Broadway.*

A global success gave founder Anita Roddick a reputation as a great business woman with a conscience. Some people confuse Body Shop with Bath & Body, which, with many locations, seems to model itself on The Body Shop. BRANCHES: across Manhattan. Tel: above number for details.

### Face Stockholm
*226 Columbus Avenue [B2]. Tel: (212) 769-1420. www.facestockholm.com*
Face is perfect for those who want to wear make-up, but look as if they aren't. The company originates in Sweden, a country known for its 'natural' beauties. BRANCHES: 110 Prince Street, Soho; Time Warner Center, Columbus Circle, Upper West Side.

### Origins
*2327 Broadway [A1]. Tel: (212) 769-0970. www.origins.com*
Like its main competitor, Aveda *(see page 87)*, Origins offers a wide range of natural eco-friendly beauty products in a feel good atmosphere. BRANCHES: across Manhattan.

## Design & Interiors

### Design Within Reach
*341 Columbus Avenue [B2]. Tel: (212) 799-5900. www.dwr.com*
Modern furniture that is functional, semi-affordable and ready-made. For those seeking sleek and fun furniture – and designed with apartment living in mind. BRANCHES: across Manhattan.

### Lightforms, Inc.
*509 Amsterdam Avenue [B1]. Tel: (212) 875-0407.*
Beaded nightlights, chandeliers, bathroom lights, floor lamps, light switch covers – it's all here; with knowledgeable and helpful staff. BRANCH: 146 West 26th Street

*Pricey perfumes.*

### Pottery Barn
*1965 Broadway [B3]. Tel: (212) 579-8477. www.potterybarn.com*
Pottery Barn joins the ranks of Crate & Barrel, Ikea, and Pier 1 to offer affordable household goods and furniture. BRANCHES: 600 Broadway, Soho; 127 East 59th Street, Upper East Side.

## Books & Music

### Bose
*10 Columbus Circle [B3]. Tel: (212) 362-7846. www.bose.com*
All your stereo and i-Pod needs at this American-made stereo store. Speakers and sound are their specialty. Their signature items include their Wave Radio and their i-Pod docking stations.

### West Side Judaica
*2412 Broadway [A1]. Tel: (212) 362-7846*
As you might imagine from the name, West Side Judaica sells all things Jewish – from books to Menorahs to gifts. If you are Jewish and need any specialty items for the holidays or if you want to come and browse, this is the place to come.

## Gifts & Souvenirs

### Avventura
*463 Amsterdam Avenue [B1]. Tel: (212) 769-2510.*

*www.forthatspecialgift.com*
This store is packed with perfect wedding gift items – vases, place settings, and linens.

**Popover's Plums**
*555 Amsterdam Avenue [B1].*
*Tel: (212) 496-9648.*
Next door to Popover's Restaurant, this gift shop seems like something from Amish country rather than the streets of New York City. For lunch or brunch or just a gift item, Popover's is worth a visit.

# Children

**Granny-Made Sweaters**
*381 Amsterdam Avenue [B2].*
*Tel: (212) 496-1222.*
Extensive collection of adorable hand-knitted and handloomed sweaters, hats, gloves, and romper-suits for children. There's an adult range of home-knits too.

**Penny Whistle Toys**
*448 Columbus Avenue [B1]. Tel: (212) 873-9090. www.pwtoys.com*
Specialists in high quality toys. A good place to come with the kids after a trip to the Museum of Natural History.

**Z'Baby Company**
*100 West 72nd Street [B2].*
*Tel: (212) 579-2229.*
*www.zbabycompany.com*
Trendy baby clothes and a few practical items at this store. The mini designer styles may seem excessive for the practically mind-ed mom and dad, but it's great for gifts for fashion-conscious parents.
BRANCH: 996 Lexington Avenue

# Food & Drink

**Barney Greengrass**
*541 Amsterdam Avenue [B1].*
*Tel: (212) 724-4707.*
*www.barneygreengrass.com*
On weekends this store/restaurant is packed with those with a craving for salmon and cream cheese bagels for brunch. The delicatessan section has a mouth-watering selection of smoked fish, caviar, jarred, and canned specialty food items. Avoid Sunday afternoons.

**Citarella**
*2135 Broadway [A2]. Tel: (212) 874-0383. www.citarella.com*
Originally a seafood specialist, Citarella has expanded into a fancy food market supplying everything you need to make a gourmet meal.
BRANCHES: across Manhattan. Tel: above number for details.

**Murray's Sturgeon Shop**
*2429 Broadway [A1].*
*Tel: (212) 724-2650.*
*www.murraysturgeon.com*
Smoked fish, rare meats, home-made salads, and a selection of caviars can all be taken to go or ordered and shipped. A long-time favorite on the Upper West Side.

**Vintage New York**
*2492 Broadway [North of map].*
*Tel: (212) 721-9999.*
*www.vintagenewyork.com*
Purveyor of wines from New York State vineyards. The staff are very knowledgeable, and there are tastings throughout the day.
BRANCH: 482 Broome Street, Soho.

**Zabar's Gourmet Foods**
*2245 Broadway [A1]. Tel: (212) 787-2000. www.zabars.com*
Eli Zabar's world-famous gourmet shop has long provided high quality fare to New Yorkers and visitors. Famous for its smoked fish and Jewish delicacies, there is also cof-fee, bread and cheese, and a range of cookware and houseware.

# Specialist

**Capezio**
*1776 Broadway, 2nd Floor [B3].*
*Tel: (212) 586-5140.*

*Inside the world-famous Zabar's.*

*www.capeziodance.com*
Traditionally a dancers' outfitter, the store now stocks exercise clothes and streetwear. Still the place to come for leotards, leg-warmers, and ballet and tap shoes.

### Lululemon
*1928 Broadway [B3]. Tel: (212) 712-1767. www.lululemon.com*
Just when it seemed the yoga craze was about to plateau, here comes high-end yoga clothing in earth-friendly fabrics and colors.

### The Shops at Columbus Circle
*10 Columbus Circle [B3].*
*Tel: (212) 823-6300.*
*www.shopsatcolumbuscircle.com*
NYC's first luxury shopping arcade. With shopping galore and plenty of food selections, including a subterranean Whole Foods – this place can entertain for hours.

## WHERE TO UNWIND

### Café La Fortuna
*69 West 71st Street [B2], tel: (212) 724-5846*
A long-time favorite among Upper Westsiders and those from other areas, this is an old-time Italian pastry shop. The décor is worn, but the outdoor garden is a nice retreat.

### Café Lalo
*201 West 83rd Street [A1], tel: (212) 496-6031*
A great place to grab a cappuccino, a late night snack or a tasty dessert. Though it gets crowded, at off times you can sit here undisturbed for hours.

### EJ's Luncheonette
*447 Amsterdam Ave [B1], tel: (212) 873-3444*
This is a 50s-style diner featuring milk shakes, French fries, and banana pancakes. The weekend brunch crowds are almost unbearable, but if you can squeeze in, you won't be disappointed with the larger-than-usual portions. Other locations across Manhattan.

### Lincoln Center
*Lincoln Center [B3], tel: (212) 546-2656*
The Lincoln Center offers many things – all in the spirit of music and dancing – but the most fun is Friday and Saturday nights in the summer when a swing band and swing dancing occupy the central outdoor courtyard – A Midsummer Night Swing. It's a great way to begin the weekend. Note that the Opera will not be operating at this location until 2009.

### Reebok Sports Club
*160 Columbus Avenue [B3], tel: (212) 362-6800*
The exclusive Reebok Gym is a great place to spoil yourself by booking a personal trainer or an appointment at the spa. Also at Rockefeller Center and East 61st Street.

# FLATIRON, UNION SQUARE, & CHELSEA

*Three varied city neighborhoods offering a range of
specialty shops and original architecture*

This chapter covers the trio of adjacent neighborhoods, the Flatiron District, Union Square, and Chelsea, that cover the central part of Manhattan between Midtown and Greenwich Village. The three are quite different from each other, and form less of a contiguous shopping area than most of the other areas in this guide, yet have enough specialty stores and other assorted places of interest to the shopper to merit inclusion.

## Union Square

So called because it marks the point at which Broadway and Fourth Avenue meet, Union Square was a fashionable place early in its history, but later became notorious for its rabble-rousing political rallies. Until the mid-1990s the square itself had deteriorated and become a hangout for vagrants, but with the advent of the market *(see below)* and a number of media-related businesses moving into the area, it is becoming fashionable again, as witnessed by such trendy restaurants as the Union Street Café (21 East 15th Street).

What really confirmed its newfound status as a shopping district was the opening in the mid-1990s of a big Barnes & Noble bookstore and later a Whole Foods market. This neighborhood's mainstays are large national and local chain stores, although it also has a smattering of some of New York's best individual stores, such as longtime residents ABC Carpet & Home and Paragon Sports, and newer outlets such as the men's clothing designer Paul Smith, and the jewelry and ethnic art shop Beads of Paradise. And with the exception of the high-end furniture stores of Tribeca, this is one of the best areas for furniture and household goods.

It's best to visit Union Square on a Monday, Wednesday, Friday, or Saturday when you can catch the excellent Greenmarket, a year-round farmers' market. Sellers come in from the country and suburbs and set up shop around the northern end of the square. Here you can find wild flowers, organic cheeses, and seasonal fruits and vegetables. Between Thanksgiving and New Year's Day the square turns into an outdoor marketplace, selling festive foods, gift items, and small selections from neighboring boutiques.

Spiraling out from Union Square, there are a number of streets to wander around, but the largest concentration of stores is on Broadway between 23rd Street and 17th Street, Fifth Avenue from 23rd to 14th, and Sixth Avenue (or Avenue of the Americas) from 14th to 23rd Streets. These streets are lined with modern chain stores in the Banana Republic, Emporio Armani vein, that have moved into the historic Ladies Mile build-

*Opposite: Union Square's 1911 Guardian Life building, one of the many early high-rises in the area. Below: ABC Carpet & Home.*

## LOCAL ATTRACTIONS

The best thing to absorb in this neighborhood is the architecture. The area includes the Flatiron District and the triangular **Flatiron Building** itself, which is at the intersection of 23rd Street and 5th Avenue. **Gramercy Park**, which you need a key to enter, is reminiscent of the gated gardens in London. Chelsea's **Joyce Theatre** is *the* dance theatre in New York, so call ahead to see who is performing; the **Union Square Theater** presents Broadway shows at an off-Broadway location. Around 28th Street, between Broadway and Lexington, you will find **Little India**, and a few blocks north is **Little Korea**, with its specialty food items and banquet-type restaurants.

ings. At the end of the 19th century, the Ladies Mile was a shopping route ranged along Broadway and Sixth Avenue. Among the notable emporia to set up shop was Lord & Taylor, which opened on Broadway in 1872 (10,000 people used its elevator in the first three days). The store moved Uptown to Fifth Avenue in 1914, where its doors are still open *(see page 22)*.

The shop buildings themselves in this area are worth the trip. In contrast to most New York stores, which are often compact and recently renovated, the stores are large and most have preserved the original architecture – a big part of this neighborhood's appeal.

### Flatiron to the Garment District

The old Flatiron District due north of Union Square is named after the spectacular Flatiron Building, located at the spot where Fifth Avenue, Broadway and 23rd Street meet. The unique triangular structure became the world's first steel-framed skyscraper when it was erected in 1902, and remains one of New York's most-photographed sights. Several other early high-rises can be seen in the area.

Other buildings hereabouts have characteristic features, such as floor-to-ceiling windows and old-fashioned elevators. This was traditionally a commercial and industrial area, and the scarcity of supermarkets, delis, and quaint little shops is a sign that residents are few and far between. Fashion, fabric, and other wholesale distributors once dominated the blocks stretching from Eighth Avenue to Fifth Avenue, north of 14th Street. Some of these businesses have been pushed out by rising rents, but there are still a number

Flatiron, Union Square and Chelsea

of wholesalers – of flowers, fabrics, and printed materials – mostly in the blocks north of 23rd Street.

The majority of these factories and showrooms are closed to the general public – only retailers are admitted. A few will open their doors to those who are most persistent or otherwise act like they know what they're talking about. Inside some of these buildings are old-time factories still in use – mostly printing presses and sewing machines cranking out material for small- to medium-size manufacturers. If you can get access to some of these places, it's a fun experience that makes you regret ever having to buy retail. The most accessible wholesaling is in the fragrant and colorful Flower District, around West 28th Street and Sixth Avenue. Enjoy an early morning stroll, when florists can be seen loading their vans with armfuls of flowers.

Thanks to its history as a printing district, you'll also find a concentration of paper and art supply shops in the area, the best of which are on West 18th Street between Fifth and Sixth Avenues.

*Year-round fresh produce at the Farmers' Market.*

## Chelsea

West of the Flatiron District between 14th and 30th Streets lies Chelsea. It encompasses the aforementioned Flower District and borders the Garment District to the north and West Village to the south. One of its most popular shopping arenas is the weekend flea market held on Sixth between 25th and 27th Streets *(see page 57)*, but the hip and happening area is West Chelsea.

Chelsea is mainly populated by young urban professionals and is the center of a big gay community, with stores reflecting that community. As rising rents forced galleries to flee Soho, they have been joined by the art, fashion, and media crowd who have found refuge in the streets west of 9th Avenue, and lately the area has come to be known as a New Soho. The pioneering Dia Center for the Arts, inaugurated in 1993, is now surrounded by contemporary galleries and artist-run spaces that have attracted equally trendy restaurants and designer stores – high-concept and high-priced Comme des Garçons on West 22nd Street is a prime example – that have moved into the old warehouses and garages.

As you head south towards the Village, look out for Chelsea Market (9th Avenue between 15th and 16th) in which dozens of food vendors and media offices are grouped together in a converted biscuit factory.

*Listings*

## Fashion & Footwear

### Anthropologie
*85 Fifth Avenue [C2].*
*Tel: (212) 627-5885.*
*www.anthropologie.com*
Casual women's fashions and housewares, from Moroccan lamps and gardening supplies to drawer pulls and children's toys.
BRANCH: 375 West Broadway.

### Diesel
*1 Union Square West [C2]. Tel: (646) 336-8552. www.diesel.com*
Considering youth fashions usually have a shelf-life of about a year, the high-concept denim and sportswear manufacturer has done well to stay at the forefront for so long. This vast flagship store has plenty of choice for the artsy and active.
BRANCH: 770 Lexington Avenue, Upper East Side.

### Intermix
*125 Fifth Avenue [C2].*
*Tel: (212) 533-9720.*
*www.intermix.com*
Stocked with up-to-the-minute women's clothing by the hottest designers, this 'Sex and the City' store is for hardened style slaves. Also has a small men's collection.
BRANCHES: 1003 Madison Av, Upper East Side; 210 Columbus Av, Upper West Side.

### J. Crew
*91 Fifth Avenue [C2]. Tel: (212) 255-4848. www.jcrew.com*
J. Crew's casual, predominantly preppy clothes never go out of fashion. Their signature khaki pants and rugby shirts keep this ever-popular store busy.
BRANCHES: across Manhattan.
Tel: above number for details.

### Jeffrey
*449 West 14th Street [A2].*
*Tel: (212) 206-1272.*
In the heart of the Meatpacking District, Jeffrey is like a mini-Barneys *(see page 32)*, stocking all the high-end designers such as Commes des Garçons, Dries Van Noten, and Jill Sander under one roof. Prices are equally high end.

### Kenneth Cole
*95 Fifth Avenue [C2]. Tel: (212) 675-2550. www.kennethcole.com*
If the shoe and leather designs don't grab your attention, Kenneth Cole's overtly political ads will. A half dozen locations throughout the city, so you can revisit something you saw first time around.
BRANCHES: across Manhattan.
Tel: 800-536-2653 for details.

### Loehmann's
*101 Seventh Avenue [B2].*
*Tel: (212) 352-0856.*
*www.loehmanns.com*
When all the department stores in New York have had their final sales and they still have items to unload, they send them over to Loehmann's. The store stocks designer clothes and shoes at drastically reduced prices.

### Lucky Brand
*172 Fifth Avenue [C1].*
*Tel: (917) 606-1418.*
*www.luckybrandjeans.com*
Casual clothing for men and women of the denim and sweatshirt variety. The store in Soho is solely devoted to kids.
BRANCHES: across Manhattan;
**Lucky Kids**: 127 Prince St, Soho.

### Old Navy
*610 Sixth Avenue [C2].*
*Tel: (212) 645-0663.*
*www.oldnavy.com*
Old Navy is part of the Gap family and sells a similar range of wardrobe staples, but at cheaper prices. It's a good place to stock up on T-shirts, but be prepared to wait in long lines outside the dressing rooms.
BRANCHES: 503 Broadway, Soho; 150 West 34th Street, Midtown.

*Opposite: All manner of accoutrements at Beads of Paradise.*

## Paul Smith

*108 Fifth Avenue [C2]. Tel: (212) 627-9770. www.paulsmith.co.uk*
British designer whose smart suits, casual wear, and accessories strike a balance between boldness and elegance. His colored pin stripes and velvet pants may be too funky for some. Good range of accessories. Men's clothes only at this store; women should head to Soho.
BRANCH: 142 Greene Street, Soho.

## Zara

*101 Fifth Avenue [C2]. Tel: (212) 741-0555. www.zara.com*
Zara's success lies in its translation of the catwalk collections into affordable clothes in record time. Good Prada lookalikes. This is the least hectic of its New York stores.
BRANCHES: 580 Broadway, Soho; 750 Lexington Av, Upper East Side; 39 West 34th Street, Midtown.

## Jewelry & Accessories

### Beads of Paradise

*16 East 17th Street [C2]. Tel: (212) 620-0642. www.beadsofparadisenyc.com*
You can string your own necklaces with first-rate beads and gems or choose from the colorful range of imported jewelry items.

## Health & Beauty

### Sephora

*119 Fifth Avenue [C2].*
*Tel: (212) 674-3570.*
*www.sephora.com*
This make-up megastore stocks practically every cosmetic designer under one roof, from funky brands such as Stilla and Urban Decay, to the more conventional Estée Lauder and Yves St. Laurent.
BRANCHES: across Manhattan.

## Design & Interiors

### ABC Carpet & Home

*888 Broadway [C2]. Tel: (212) 473-3000. www.abchome.com*
There are two ABCs adjacent to each other – one for carpets and the other for everything else for your home, from home-entertainment systems to floor pillows, and lamps to baby basinets.

### Bed, Bath & Beyond

*620 Sixth Avenue [C2]. Tel: (212) 255-3550. www.bedbathandbeyond.com*
What began as a chain store devoted to the bedroom and bathroom, has recently been putting more emphasis on the 'beyond' and now stocks kitchenware as well as selected foodstuffs.
BRANCH: 410 East 61st Street, Upper East Side.

### The Container Store

*629 Sixth Avenue [B2]. Tel: (212) 366-4200. www.containerstore.com*
If you are craving organization in your life, this is the place to

**TIP**
ABC, the furniture and carpet emporium, has an outlet store in the Bronx. If you can make your way up there – the Broadway store can give you directions – you will find things at 30–50 percent off the main store's prices. The selection isn't as great, but the quality is just as good.

*Listings*

*Barnes & Noble's flagship store, Union Square.*

**TIP**
Just north of 23rd Street begins the world of wholesale warehouses and stores, dealing in flowers, furniture, clothing, and decorative items. Most of these stores are closed to ordinary customers, but some you can talk your way into. The main thoroughfare of the flower market is 28th Street between Seventh Avenue and Broadway. Much of the furniture and fabric world is centered around Fifth Avenue between 34th Street and 23rd Street – and there are lots of other things in between.

come. From plastic storage bins, to pencil cases, to closet systems to wrapping paper. This store will help you hide your chaos.
BRANCH: 725 Lexington Avenue.

### Country Home & Comfort
*43 West 22nd Street [C1].*
*Tel: (212) 675-2705.*
'From rural comfort to urban sophistication' is this furniture store's tag-line. It's so comfortable you will want to take a break here.

### Home Depot
*40 West 23rd Street [C1].*
*Tel: (212) 929-9571.*
*www.homedepot.com*
A glorified hardware store that makes even a novice feel competent at home improvement. The store also carries outdoor furniture, carpets, and kitchen appliances.
BRANCH: across New York City.

### Imports from Marrakesh
*88 Tenth Avenue [A2].*
*Tel: (212) 675-9700.*
Between the food halls of Chelsea Market, this Moroccan design shop, with its mosaic tables, mirrors, and ornate lanterns, stands out among its neighbors.

### Les Migrateurs
*200 Lexington Avenue [off map]. Tel: (212) 966-8208.*
*www.lesmigrateurs*
Les Migrateurs has migrated to New York from Paris, but it is at

home here with the European furniture stores in this neighborhood.

### Olde Good Things
*124 West 24th Street [B1].*
*Tel: (212) 989-8401.*
*www.oldegoodthings.com*
This furniture store has dubbed itself the 'place of architecturologists.' Pretentious perhaps, but the selection stretches beyond the usual antique shop fare, and includes fireplace mantels, barber-shop chairs, and other unusual pieces.

### Restoration Hardware
*935 Broadway [C2].*
*Tel: (212) 260-9479.*
*www.restorationhardware.com*
Reclaims past products – from Bon Ami scouring detergents, to glow-in-the-dark ceiling stars, to Mission-style furniture. Old styles repackaged with modern flair.

### Sam Flax
*12 West 20th [C2]. Tel: (212) 620-3038. www.samflaxny.com*
Office supplies galore, including desk chairs, pens and paper, artists can also find canvases and paints.
BRANCH: 900 Third Avenue.

## Books, Music, & Electronics

### B&H Photo-Video
*420 Ninth Avenue [N of B1].*
*Tel: (212) 444-5041.*

*www.bhphotovideo.com*
Professionals and amateurs are catered for here – from films and lenses to flash-guns and lighting equipment. Run by Orthodox Jews and adheres to a strict religious calendar – closed before sundown on Friday and all day Saturday.

**Barnes & Noble**
*33 East 17th Street [C2].*
*Tel: (212) 253-0810.*
*www.barnesandnoble.com*
Of all the chain bookstore locations in Manhattan, this is the most pleasant to sit in. It's also one of the largest; in addition to books, it stocks cards and stationery and has an excellent music section.
BRANCHES: across Manhattan.

**Circuit City**
*52–64 East 14th Street [C2].*
*Tel: (212) 387-0730.*
*www.circuitcity.com*
Circuit City can take care of all of your electronics needs, and – because there is plenty of competition for these items – they are usually willing to offer the cheapest price, if you can prove that somewhere else is selling it for less.
BRANCHES: 232–240 East 86th Street, Upper East Side; 2232 Broadway, Upper West Side.

**Virgin Megastore**
*52 East 14th Street [C2].*
*Tel: (212) 598-4666.*
*www.virginmega.com*
Open 365 days a year, this British music megastore has a broad range, with listening posts to sample new sounds. Also stocks books, videos, and computer games.
BRANCH: 1540 Broadway.

# Children

## Books of Wonder
*18 West 18th Street [C2].*
*Tel: (212) 989-3270.*
*www.booksofwonder.com*

This shop has row upon row of children's books. It organizes guest appearances by local and renowned authors.

**Schneider's**
*41 West 25th Street [C1].*
*Tel: (212) 228-3540.*
This family-run store carries all the major brands in baby products, and the owners are always on hand to answer questions.

## Food, Drink, & Plants

**Chelsea Garden Center**
*499 Tenth Avenue [off map].*
*Tel: (212) 727-7100.*
Sells not only beautiful planters and flowers, but also unique outdoor and indoor furniture.
BRANCH: 455 West 16th Street.

**Chelsea Market**
*75 Ninth Avenue [A2].*
*www.chelseamarket.com.*
A series of food halls and eateries in a converted biscuit factory. Includes a grocery shop for fish,

*The busy B&H store is popular with pros and beginners.*

*Listings*

meat, wine, Italian specialties, and other gourmet goodies. For a complete list of shops, see the website.

**Italian Wine Merchants**
*108 East 16th Street [C2].*
*Tel: (212) 473-2323.*
*www.italianwinemerchants.com*
Take advantage of the owners' expertise and treat yourself to some specialty Italian wines. Try to catch one of their wine-tasting sessions.

**New York Cake & Bake Supplies**
*56 West 22nd Street [C1]. Tel: (212) 675-2253. www.nycake.com*
Rolling pins, cake molds, cookie cutters and anything else one might need for baking.

**T. Salon and Emporium**
*Chelsea Market, 75 Ninth Avenue [A2]. Tel: (212) 358-0506. www.tsalon.com*
Pick up a teapot and an exotic tea or while away the hours sipping a tea.

**Union Square Green Market**
*Union Square [C2].*
A local farmers' market takes over the northern end of Union Square Park on Monday, Wednesday, Friday and Saturday; fresh flowers, eggs, fish, and seasonal produce.

## Specialist

**Paper Access**
*23 West 18th Street [C2].*
*Tel: (212) 463-7035*
Everything from fancy cards to paper by the pound in every color. Cards to buy or make your own.

**Paragon**
*867 Broadway [C2].*
*Tel: (212) 255-8036.*
*www.paragonsports.com*
One-stop shopping for all your sporting needs – from skis to tennis socks to golf clubs.

**The Shop at Equinox**
*897 Broadway [C2].*
*Tel: (212) 780-9300.*
*www.equinoxfitness.com*
Exercise equipment store with a range of pants and tops.

**TIP**

If you're visiting New York at Christmas time, there is an outdoor market/craft fair assembled in the middle of Union Square. It usually stays up from Thanksgiving through Christmas, and offers some great handmade items as well as collections from several neighboring stores.

---

### WHERE TO UNWIND

**Blow**
*342 West 14th Street [B2]. Tel: (212) 989-6282. www.xoblow.com*
For those who want others to blow and style their hair and who can't get an appointment or don't want to deal with the hassle.

**Chelsea Piers**
*Pier 62, West Side Highway/23rd Street [A1/2] Tel: (212) 336-6666. www.chelseapiers.com*
A bowling alley, a driving range, sailing classes, a full service gym with yoga and dance classes, a skating rink, gymnastic classes...what doesn't Chelsea Piers have? Unwind with the activity of your choice, then grab a drink and a bite at the Brewery.

**Empire Diner**
*210 Tenth Avenue [A1]*
*Tel: (212) 243-2736*

This diner is a New York landmark. In addition to the standard diner fare, its offerings of mozzarella and basil salad, and fresh squeezed lemonade, put it a notch above the rest. Open 24 hours.

**71 Irving Place**
*71 Irving Place [C2]*
*Tel: (212) 995-5252*
A bit off the beaten path, just south of peaceful Gramercy Park, this is a nice place to relax over a cup of coffee or tea, and some pastries. Occasional live music.

**The City Bakery**
*3 West 18th Street [C2]*
*Tel: (212) 366-1414*
Often bustling, this is a great place to have lunch or an afternoon snack. Look out for the extra-tempting 'chocolate room.'

# Flea Markets & Street Fairs

*Look for unusual clothes, good-quality rugs, and fresh foodstuffs at
these outdoor venues, or just mingle with the crowds*

**W**hen the warm weather hits, many empty lots or weekday parking
lots turn into flea markets for the weekend. Life in the crowded
city isn't conducive to all those garage sales the suburbs are
famous for, so instead people bring all their goods to the long-established
markets that exist in most neighborhoods. The most notable ones in
Manhattan are at Avenue A and East 11th Street in the East Village, at Sixth
Avenue and West 25th/26th Street in Chelsea, and at Columbus Avenue and
West 77th Street on the Upper West Side. There is usually something going
on at summer weekends on Sixth Avenue below 14th Street, at Bleecker and
Leroy in the West Village, and at East 67th Street between York and First
Avenue on the Upper East Side.

## Quality Control

Sellers at these markets must have a permit. This ensures that consumers are
buying from committed sellers and not being taken for a ride. It also helps to
ensure some level of quality control. What is sold varies from vendor to vendor and location to location, but all markets have a wide range of goods.
Most carry large quantities of furniture and carpets, clothing, toys, and
games. Some are open all year round, but you certainly get a better selection,
plus a more pleasant shopping experience, if you happen to be there in
spring, summer or early fall.

*Keep an
eye out for
bargains at
New York's
street fairs.*

On most Saturdays and Sundays
in these warmer seasons, it's common for one avenue or another to be
closed off to commercial traffic
because of a street fair. Whilst this is
aggravating to motorists and
pedestrians trying to navigate their
way around them, it means those
who have come to enjoy the fairs
can wander for blocks and absorb
whatever it is they are offering without having to worry about traffic.
Vendors of all kinds are lined up one
after the other for up to 10 blocks.
Food is the most common feature –
typical fare includes corn on the
cob, fresh-squeezed lemonade, and
grilled sausages.

What else is sold in the street fairs
is really a hodgepodge of goods –
discounted socks and underwear,
Balinese mirrors and masks, vinyl
LPs, hand-made jewelry and handbags. The only consistent element
seems to be the cheap prices.

# THE EAST VILLAGE & THE LOWER EAST SIDE

*They're next-door neighbors, distinctively New York in character, yet they remain worlds apart in shadow and substance*

I f you're into used clothing and high on tattoos and piercings, the East Village is for you. Its heyday was of course the late 1960s and early '70s, when everybody who was anybody was turning on and tuning in to the anti-war and civil-rights protests. The joint was indeed jumpin' and attracting a good deal of notoriety. Things have simmered down a bit – though not too much. Now there's hip-hop and grunge music, and in the East Village you can still find the largest concentration of tattoo and piercing parlors, used-clothing stores and record and music shops. These are the boundaries: Lafayette Street to the west, the East River to the east, 14th Street to the north and Canal Street to the south, with Houston (pronounced HOW-stun) Street being the neighborhood's biggest thoroughfare. It's the neighborhood you were once warned about, especially the part once known as Alphabet City, in which the streets change from numbers to letters (avenues A, B, C, and D). The place is gentrifying rapidly, but people still come here to get their knishes and pastrami sandwiches and observe the kids jumping rope under Grandma's watchful eye as she counts along in Spanish. The immigrant cycle spirals on in New York. There was a big Hispanic influx here, primarily people from the Dominican Republic and Puerto Rico seeking economic opportunity in the Big Apple and environs. There's a blend of old and new, and life seems to move at a slower pace here – especially on Sundays and Mondays when many stores are closed.

## Changing Times

As rents rise, new shops emerge. They're more polished, more hip. Meanwhile, teetering on the edge of bankruptcy are some of the Polish delis, Dominican cake shops and decades-old stationery stores. Rent-stabilized and rent-controlled apartments have helped residents continue to call this neighborhood home, but many are being replaced by younger New Yorkers, either those who have just moved here after graduating from college to start careers, or those who work in the music, film, and publishing industries. This helps to explain the number of trendy and used-clothing stores, and also the density of music-related stores and venues (*see page 69*).

In your wanderings around the East Village, you may also be struck by the number of body piercings and tattooed faces – this is the center for grunge, bohemian, and alternative cultures. Tattoo and piercing parlors rival the number of music stores. If you're inspired by all of the tattoos and piercings you witness, you can easily duck into one of these shops, many of which can be found along St. Mark's Place, the neighborhood's main thoroughfare.

*Opposite: Black remains the color of choice in the East Village. Below: Center for artists and other bohemian types.*

To avoid confusion, St. Mark's is the same as East 8th Street. As far as other street names go, this neighborhood can be confusing since its street names, which run east-west, are the same as the avenue names (running north-south). Be sure to clarify if someone is talking about First Avenue or 1st Street, and remember that in New York names of avenues are spelled out (as in Fifth Avenue) while names of streets are rendered with numerals (5th Street).

Besides the high concentration of stores on St. Mark's Place, the most popular zones are along 5th and 9th streets – both with rather more in the way of boutiques. And on almost every block there's a community garden, a welcome respite from the usual pattern of stores, restaurants, and apartment buildings. These gardens are a source of constant struggle between the residents and the Mayor's office, which would like to get rid of them in favor of more lucrative real estate deals.

## The Lower East Side

To the south of Houston is the Lower East Side, an area in transition and the other chief focus of this chapter. There has sometimes been confusion over the East Village vis-à-vis the Lower East Side, but they're really quite different. Walking down Clinton Street on the Lower East Side, for

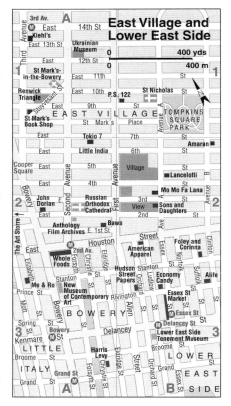

East Village and Lower East Side

## LOCAL ATTRACTIONS

This diverse neighborhood is home to cultural experiences, including **off-Broadway theaters** such as the Kabul Theater, P.S. 122, the East 13th Street Theater, St. Mark's Church and Theater, and La MaMa. New York's Public Theater hosts each summer its famous Shakespeare In The Park: two Shakespeare productions performed in the Public's outdoor theater in Central Park. (Contact the Public Theater about getting free tickets or about how to pay for other Public produced events, many of which make their way to Broadway, or across the country.) There is also the **Anthology Film Archives**, which screens works-in-progress, and completed documentaries.

To get an idea of what life was like for the Irish, East European, and Jewish immigrants who crowded into this area in the 19th century, visit the **Lower East Side Tenement Museum**. The **Eldridge Street Synagogue** is a grand Moorish-style landmark, built in 1887 and now restored. This was the focal point of the once large Jewish community of the area. To see where we are heading, stop at **The New Museum**, a new addition on Bowery.

*Street lamp art at the East Village's St. Mark's Place.*

instance, you'll find smart new fashion boutiques next to some random home appliance store or Dominican cake shop. The Lower East Side has resisted gentrification to a greater extent, and you can still find more than the usual number of Jewish delicatessens, small neighborhood temples and Stars of David on the facades of buildings. And even where the trendy stores have popped up, they are often situated right next to the furniture store or the nail salon that have been serving local residents for decades.

The Lower East Side, more than any other neighborhood in Manhattan, gives you a sense of the New York that was home to waves of immigrants. There's even a Tenement Museum to remind us what living conditions were like for those fleeing persecution, hard times, the military draft, or whatever else. Over the past few years, boutiques – and many more restaurants – have opened up along Clinton, Ludlow, Orchard, Stanton, and Rivington, the area's main shopping streets. The farther south, especially once you cross Delancey, the more local the businesses get, though that is rapidly changing.

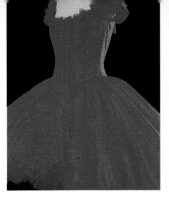

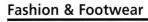

*Beautiful gowns from Mary Adams.*

**TIP**

The concept of public restrooms has never really caught on in New York. Your best bet is to find a large or department store. In some cases you will have to request a key. Other possibilities are hotel lobbies, fast food joints, coffee shops, and, of course, Starbucks.

## Fashion & Footwear

### Alife Rivington Club
*158 Rivington Street [B3].*
*Tel: (212) 375-8128.*
*www.rivingtonclub.com*
A sneaker boutique. Dark wood paneled display cases, high security, discreet presentation...and very fashionable sneakers.

### Alpana Bawa
*70 East 1st Street [A2].*
*Tel: (212) 254-1249.*
*www.alpanabawa.com*
The clothing at Bawa is fabulous if you're looking for something out of the ordinary – designs include men's cotton shirts with embroidery, women's silk tops in bright oranges and fuchsias, and wool-and-silk dresses.

### American Apparel
*183 Houston Street [B2].*
*Tel: (212) 598-4600.*
*www.americanapparel.net*
The ads and attitude are far trendier than the wares being sold – T-shirts in every color of the rainbow. Though some styles change to match the current trends; others stay the same. Other clothing items and accessories also on sale.
BRANCHES: across Manhattan.

### Anna
*150 East 3rd Street [B2].*
*Tel: (212) 358-0195.*

The success of owner Kathy's own line means that her innovative womenswear – from wrap T-shirts to tight dresses – dominates the store, with lines from local designers too.

### Foley and Corinna
*108 Stanton Street [B2].*
*Tel: (212) 529-2338.*
*www.foleyandcorinna.com*
A stylish range of women's clothing combining fancy and funky designs by Dana Foley with top-notch vintage clothing by Anna Corinna. There is a man's store around the corner on Ludlow.

### Mary Adams
*138 Ludlow Street [B3].*
*Tel: (212) 473-0237.*
*www.maryadamsthedress.com*
This designer works in silk, velvet and layered sheer to create beautiful made-to-order and off-the-rack women's evening- and bridalwear.

### Mo Mo Fa Lana
*43 Avenue A [B2].*
*Tel: (212) 979-9595.*
*www.momofalana.com*
Hand-painted silks and cashmere are what make this East Village staple so famous. The designs are similar to tie-dye, but on finer fabrics. The clothing here has hence earned itself quite a fancy reputation, and has been profiled in all of the major fashion magazines.

### Shop
*105 Stanton Street [B3].*
*Tel: (212) 375-0304.*
*www.iloveshop.com*
This was one of the first shops to gentrify this previously rather downmarket neighborhood. You can find clothing by Jill Stuart, Cosabella, and other mid- to high-end designers, plus some that are unique to Shop.

### Steven by Steve Madden
*100 Rivington Street [B3].*
*Tel: (212) 387-7924.*
*www.stevemadden.com*
This high-end shoe store is a new and controversial addition to the Lower East Side. A part of a mega-chain selling trendy and expensive shoes, locals worry that this opening is a sign of the changing times.

### Tokio 7
*64 East 7th Street [A2].*
*Tel: (212) 353-8443.*
To catch your attention, this resale/consignment shop usually has a Prada dress featured in the window. Once inside, you will find a vast range of men's and women's designer wear, with most items looking as good as new.

### Vui Vui
*309 East 9th Street [A1].*
*Tel: (212) 598-9836.*
Everything on sale in this shop – from the men's and women's clothes to the purses and small kitchenware range – is made in Vietnam. They do great combinations of metal and fabrics, such as cloth bags with iron handles or linen tops with metal buttons on the shoulders.

## Health & Beauty

### Fragrance Shop New York, Inc.
*21 East 7th Street [A2].*
*Tel: (212) 254-8950.*
*www.fragranceshopnewyork.com*
This place does perfumes for men, women, and the home, plus oils and other bath products. Be prepared for an olfactory overload, though – as there are so many different fragrances here.

### Kiehl's
*109 Third Avenue [A1].*
*Tel: (212) 677-3171.*
*www.kiehls.com*
You get the impression of being in a traditional apothecary when wandering among the old-fashioned-looking shampoos, soaps, shaving items, and other beauty products in the Kiehl's line. The acclaimed range is now found in department stores and sold internationally, and it's a big favorite among the celebrity crowd.

## Design & Interiors

### Amaran
*109 Avenue B [B2].*
*Tel: (212) 420-0427.*
*www.amaran.com*
Amaran sell Balinese couches, silver jewelry from the Far East, brightly colored silky pillows, and other pretty things to decorate your home and yourself.

*Thrift shops: for bohos and bargain hunters.*

## Billy's Antiques and Props

*76 East Houston Street [A2]. Tel: (917) 576-6980. www.billysantiques.com*
Popular with collectors, businesses, and movie producers, Billy's stocks an interesting array of hand-picked antiques and props, including New York City street signs, old-fashioned bath-tubs, and household appliances.

## Bodanna: Ceramics
## Studio & Gallery

*125 East 7th Street [B2]. Tel: (212) 388-0078. www.bodanna.org*
This studio-cum-gallery sells ceramic mugs, bowls, vases, and plates that are produced on the premises. Items are simple, in modest colors that should go with everything. The studio also teaches pottery to young adults on a low income and offers more general pottery classes.

## Harris Levy

*98 Forsyth Street [A3]. Tel: (212) 226-3102. www.harrislevy.com*
Since 1894 this firm has been selling fine linens, top-quality sheets, dish towels, and wonder-fully thick bath towels. Most items come at a price, although less extravagant shoppers will find modest items too.

## John Derian Company, Inc.

*6 East 2nd Street [A2]. Tel: (212) 677-3917. www.johnderian.com*
Peering into this shop, you might mistake it for someone's private home. The place gives a pretty good indication of how welcoming your own home could look if it were enhanced with some of John Derian's Parisian pillow-cases, Turkish lanterns, or their signature decoupage.
BRANCH: **John Derian Dry Goods**, 10 East 2nd Street.

## Lancelotti Housewares

*66 Avenue A [B2]. Tel: (212) 475-6851.*
This store's 1950s-style logo is emblematic of the retro-inspired designer items it sells. The furry floor pillows, bed and bath linens, plastic tables and moulded chairs, rechargeable lamps – all are typi-cal of the housewares that grace stylish East Village apartments.

## La Sirena

*27 East 3rd Street [A2]. Tel: (212) 780-9113. www.lasirenanyc.com*
A splash of Mexico in the heart of Manhattan. Ornate silver frames and crosses, brightly coloured ornaments, hand-painted pottery, carved figures and a lovely range of handbags and baskets are just

*All you need for a close shave at Kiehl's.*

*A world of books at the local independent bookstore.*

some of the traditional Mexican artifacts packed into the store.

# Books & Music

### Bluestockings
*172 Allen Street [B3].*
*Tel: (212) 777-6028. www.blue-stockings.com*
Bluestockings functions as a café and a community space as well as a bookstore. If you are looking for books with a feminist focus, this is the place to come. It also hosts readings by well-known authors.

### St. Mark's Book Shop
*31 Third Avenue [A1].*
*Tel: (212) 260-7853.*
*www.stmarksbookshop.com*
This independent bookstore has an impressive collection, with a focus on art books, literary journals, and progressive non-fiction.

# Gifts & Souvenirs

### Alphabets
*115 Avenue A [B1].*
*Tel: (212) 475-7250.*
*www.alphabetsny.com*
This store manages to make souvenir items – including T-shirts, magnets, and tote bags –

look cute, and they also carry a range of affordable gift items.
BRANCHES: 47 Greenwich Avenue, Greenwich Village.

### Lower East Side
### Tenement Museum Shop
*108 Orchard Street [B3].*
*Tel: (212) 431-0233.*
*www.tenement.org*
The museum shop is a great place to buy historical books and contemporary gift items made by the ethnic communities that still dominate the Lower East Side. If you have time, a visit to the museum itself is worthwhile.

# Children

### Crembebe
*68 Second Avenue [A2].*
*Tel: (212) 979-6848.*
*www.crembebe.com*
Crembébé stocks clothes for infants and toddlers by French designers; some appear almost too precious to wear, while others will work for the most accident-prone child. The store itself is as cute as some of the clothing – an indoor space made to look like an outside yard, and there's even a fence for the salesclerk to peer over.

### Dinosaur Hill
*306 East 9th Street [A1].*
*Tel: (212) 473-5850.*
*www.dinosaurhill.com*
Dinosaur Hill is full of children's toys, puzzles, and mobiles to keep kids busy while their parents shop.

### Little Stinkers Shoe Company
*280 East 10th Street [B1].*
*Tel: (212) 253-0282.*
The great range of shoes here means that you can satisfy both their children's footwear needs and their desires. Shoes from practical to fanciful.

*Listings*

*Below: Read all about it in any good book store.*

*Below Right: Sweet heaven at Economy Candy.*

### Sons and Daughters
*35 Avenue A [C2].*
*Tel: (212) 253-7797.*
This fun and fancy children's store is a little on the expensive side, but its merchandise, carefully selected from around the world, is irresistible.

## Food & Drink

### Doughnut Plant
*379 Grand Street [B3].*
*Tel: (212) 505-3700.*
*www.doughnutplant.com*
You have to get up early to enjoy these 'healthy' doughnuts – the store only stays open until the supply of doughnuts runs out. The organic and natural ingredients deceive you into thinking that eating doughnuts is good for you.

### Economy Candy
*108 Rivington Street [B3].*
*Tel: (212) 254-1531.*
*www.economycandy.com*
If you need to buy candy in bulk, or have a hankering for some unusual European candy bar or dried fruit, this is as good a place as any to find it.

### Essex Street Market
*120 Essex Street [B3].*
*Tel: (212) 388-0449.*
*www.essexstreetmarket.com*

A local favorite, this is similar to an indoor farmer's market, plus a real taste of the Lower East Side. Everything from fancy cheese shops to clothing stalls to Jeffrey's meat market; and sushi for lunch.

### Il Laboratorio del Gelato
*95 Orchard Street [B3].*
*Tel: (212) 343-9922.*
*www.illaboratoriodelgelato.com*
Earl Grey, Malt, Chocolate Basil, this isn't your average ice cream shop, but one catering to those with a discerning palate. If you can't make it to the store, they sell their gelato to several fine restaurants around Manhattan.

### Porto Rico Coffee Company
*40½ St. Mark's Place (aka East 8th St) [A1]. Tel: (212) 533-1982*
This company produces some of the best coffee in the world. Sample one of their many rich blends while you wait for them to grind up a supply to take home.
BRANCHES: 201 Bleecker Street, Greenwich Village; 107 Thompson Street, Soho.

## Specialist

### Autumn Skateboard Shop
*436 East 9th Street [B1].*
*Tel: (212) 677-6220.*
This place stocks everything for

the skateboarder from a wide range of boards, many of which are works of art in themselves, to knee pads, wallets, and T-shirts.

## Babeland
*94 Rivington Street [B3].*
*Tel: (212) 375-1701.*
*www.babeland.com*
An adult toy store, this shop specializes in female sexual pleasure and the very knowledgeable staff can direct you to appropriate items to overcome any sexual uncertainty.
BRANCH: 43 Mercer Street.

## Blick Art Materials
*1 Bond Street [Arrowed off map]*
*Tel: (212) 533-2444.*
*www.dickblick.com*
Easels, paint brushes, paints, pencils – this store can supply all your artistic needs. It also has a tasteful range of note cards, wrapping paper, and picture frames.

## Chef Restaurant
*294 Bowery [A2].*
*Tel: (212) 254-6644.*
This store caters mostly to restaurant suppliers, but chef wannabes can purchase all manner of cooking necessities – baking sheets, strainers, knives, etc. – and all at a discount. There are several stores identical to this one on Bowery.

## Downtown Yarns
*45 Avenue A [B2].*
*Tel: (212) 995-5991.*
With the surge in popularity of knitting there are now a handful of stores in New York City specializing in knitting supplies. This one has a variety of yarns, in all thicknesses and colors, and needles of all sizes. There's the bonus of a dedicated, knowledgeable staff.

## Hudson Street Papers
*149 Orchard Street [B3].*
*Tel: (212) 229-1064.*
You can buy books, wrapping paper, and gifts for almost every occasion here.

*Manhattan Portage, for practical hard-wearing bags.*

## KD Dance
*339 Lafayette Street [Soho map B1]. Tel: (212) 533-1037.*
*www.kddance.com*
The clothes here are designed specifically for dancing and exercizing, but look so good they can be worn anywhere.

## Manhattan Portage Stores
*335 East 9th Street [A1].*
*Tel: (212) 995-5490.*
If you need heavy-duty but good-looking bags to transport your goods home in, Manhattan Portage, whose bags were originally designed for bike messengers, should be able to help.
BRANCH: 301 West Broadway.

## Surma
*11 East 7th Street [A1].*
*Tel: (212) 477-0729.*
This Ukrainian shop carries traditional clothing and gift items such as hand-painted wooden eggs.

*Clinton Street Bakery.*

## WHERE TO UNWIND

### Clinton Street Bakery
*4 Clinton Street [B2]*
*Tel: (646) 602-6263*
This company's freshly baked goods are sold in other locations throughout New York City, but it's best to come to the source. It's also a great breakfast, lunch, or early-dinner spot, and popular with the local crowd.

### Il Buco
*47 Bond Street [A2]*
*Tel: (212) 533-1932*
Il Buco used to be an antique store by day and restaurant by night, but these days it's just a restaurant. The menu offers tapas and Italian dishes, so you can either nibble on a few things or enjoy a complete meal. Accompany your food with wine from the carefully chosen list.

### Mitali East
*334 East 6th Street [A2]*
*Tel: (212) 533-2508*
This is only one of a dozen or so Indian restaurants that you can find on this 6th Street block between First and Second Avenues – an area that has been dubbed 'Little India.' We recommend this one but all the restaurants serve up tasty Indian treats, and some even have live music and dancing.

### Whole Foods Market
*95 East Houston Street [A2]*
*Tel: (212) 420-1320*
The second floor of this beyond average grocery store has a sushi bar, salad bar, and pasta eatery. You can also purchase food in the market and then bring it upstairs to eat and relax. There is free wireless and a good number of places to sit and relax, so come and decompress.

### 10th Street Baths
*268 East 10th Street [B1]*
*Tel: (212) 674-9250*
At these Russian and Turkish-style baths you can get fully lathered up or just come for a steam. Telephone to check on the sessions before visiting – some nights are gender specific (Wednesday ladies only).

# The Music Scene

*The East Village and Lower East Side record shops and clubs are alive with the sound of music, where fans seek out the next big thing*

**M**usicians and music lovers should head straight for the East Village and the Lower East Side, where practically every block has a record shop, live music venue, or instrument store. The area has long been popular with fans of alternative music, and whenever a genre or a band is perceived to have sold out and gone mainstream, East Village audiences lead the search for something different, flocking to the smaller clubs to watch up-and-coming acts strut their stuff. A lot of now-legendary bands paid their dues here: Ani DiFranco, Luscious Jackson, the Talking Heads, Patti Smith, and the Ramones, to name but a few.

Most of the stores sell vinyl LPs, new and used – and are reminiscent of John Cusack's Chicago record shop in *High Fidelity*. In fact, it's hard to think of any other place on earth where there is such a concentration of these stores, this in a world in which record players have become largely outmoded for at least the past decade. DJs form the main clientele. Most focus on a specific genre: reggae for Jammyland, funk and R&B for A-1 Records; usually there are DJs spinning records in the front or back of the store. The same goes for other music stores, equally common in this part of town. For the novice, some of these places can be intimidating, giving off a certain 'members only' attitude. But once the ice is broken you'll generally find store clerks – who are usually the owners themselves – helpful.

Where there isn't a music shop, there's likely to be a store selling musical equipment – new, vintage, custom-built, or refurbished. These stores offer repair services, too. Of course, there are other places throughout New York where you can buy music and related goods. There are still a few surviving CD stores, the most comprehensive is Virgin on 14th Street, but most Barnes & Noble branches have a music section. This might be one instance where the smaller, niche specific shops outlived the mega-store. But things are different on the Lower East Side, and it's unlikely that one of these larger stores would make much of a dent here. The neighborhood shops have a loyal following, and besides, their collections really can't be duplicated. However, if you are looking for top 40 selections, head to the bigger stores – or risk being convinced otherwise by a hipster on the Lower East Side.

Sam Ash – which takes up half a block in the middle of Manhattan, is probably the largest seller of musical equipment. But be warned that these guys are looking to seal the deal rather than build a lasting relationship. They will make lots of promises, but if you don't want to be rushed and have lots of questions, Rivington Guitars, Ludlow Guitars, and other places on the Lower East Side are the way to go.

Check out *The Village Voice*, *The Onion*, *Time Out*, or similar papers offering listings of 'what's happening.' It's likely that the music section will point you to Mercury Lounge, Bowery Ballroom, Arlene Grocery, or one of the other venues in this part of town. Sadly, the venue that started it all, CBGB's was forced out of business due to rising rents. Most venues and artists cater to a younger audience; if you aren't part of that age group but can handle a loud bar, take a chance and it's likely that you won't be disappointed.

# GREENWICH VILLAGE

*Along with the customary exotica, this popular old haunt's
wide range of shops has something for everyone*

This is Manhattan's original hippie heaven, now approaching a century's worth of fame as such. The neighborhood has long been a popular shopping destination, as distinct from some of the newer, flash-in-the-pan attractions, which are either freshly concocted to pull in the tourists or simply experiencing a renaissance or gentrification.

In the good old days before double-ID requirements, Greenwich Village was the place young people from the boonies (the sticks) came to for drinking purposes, the place where newly arrived tourists shopped by day and gawked by night at same-sex dancing partnerships in bars and clubs. Along came the Beatniks in the late 1950s to start ratcheting up the Village's idiosyncratic persona, congregating in cafés to dig the new sounds in poetry and jazz. Today the New York University students and the teens that come here from other neighborhoods try to recapture that hallowed 1960s attitude.

The bohemian image is reflected in store windows, but much of this densely-packed neighborhood has expanded its repertoire and caters these days to the tastes of a broader range of people. It's also the place to come if you have a hobby – like fanatics of chess and board games, connoisseurs of rare books, gardeners, avid letter writers. Their needs are met here. Put it this way: whereas the East Village deals with the stirrings of a younger set and the Upper East Side with a more elitist crowd, the Village is for all – young and old, rich and poor, bohemian and bourgeois. It also remains the best place in New York City to hear good jazz.

## Points of Reference

The first thing you want to do is avoid getting lost. There's no neat grid plan with numbered streets here as there is further north in Manhattan, so buyer beware. Make careful note of street names and locations. Even lifetime New Yorkers consider it a challenge to navigate. Some streets last for only a block, others change name in mid-block. And most streets crisscross at odd angles. Bleecker Street, the Village's main drag, runs practically in an east/west semicircle. At one point, West 12th Street is steps away from West 4th Street. Don't confuse Greenwich Avenue and Greenwich Street – their intersection probably earned the neighborhood its moniker as Greenwich Village.

At the epicenter is Washington Square Park, often crowded with kids playing hackiesack (ball) and men playing chess. If you're a pedestrian passing through, watch out for skateboarders and drug dealers, though often the dealers are in fact plain-clothes police officers in disguise.

## Life in the Mews Lane

The big institution down here is New York University, which borders Washington Square Park on all sides. If you want a shopping distraction, the famous Mews Houses on the northeastern corner offer a sample of some old and rare New York architecture. (The

*Opposite:
Christopher
Street is the
gay center of
New York.
Below: Quirky
design at
Fassbinder.*

Upper East Side and Murray Hill are the only other neighborhoods fortunate enough to have Mews Houses, most of which were long ago converted to residential homes and artists' studios.) You can walk down this alley and even peer in at some of the houses, owned by fortunate NYU professors and administrators. North of Washington Square Park is University Place, one of your best bets when it comes to unique New York shops. With the exception of 8th Street, which is big on shoe stores, the streets running east-west offer little in the way of shopping. But the renovated brownstones, especially those along 9th and 10th Streets, have long caught peoples' attention. Out front you might find visitors remarking on their beauty, or perhaps starstruck fans waiting for celebrities to pass by – Julia Roberts, Tim Robbins and Susan Sarandon, Ed Norton, and Richard Gere all keep apartments here.

To the east and west of Washington Square Park are Broadway and Sixth Avenue respectively, each offering the standard fare of chain stores and trendy teen stores, one indistinguishable from the next, with the same T-shirts, pants and dresses, albeit with different labels and only slightly different styles. Sixth Avenue is home to one of New York's oldest and best-known stores – Bigelow's Apothecary. This is where Balducci's Market was located for almost 100 years, now replaced with Citarella's located on 8th Street.

South of Washington Square the streets are crowded with rather nondescript stores, often open late, cheek by jowl with 24-hour coffee shops and cheap restaurants. After raunchy Times Square was Disneyfied and sanitized by high-rent developers, the fake ID stores, tattoo parlors and 'head shops'

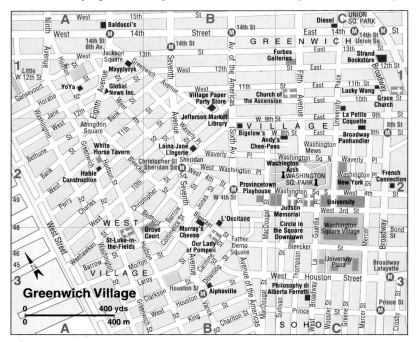

Greenwich Village

picked up stakes and moved to The Village. This section is a big departure from the quaintness of the West Village, which begins on the other side of Seventh Avenue.

## The West Village and the Meatpacking District

In the West Village you can wander along cobblestoned and tree-lined streets where the buildings are rarely taller than five storys. Here the stores are inviting – flower boxes in windows and bells on doors. This area has long been known for its downhome boutiques. But with the opening of the ultra-chic Marc Jacobs stores on Bleecker Street, the area is going the Soho route and turning pricey and designer-driven. Neighbors were resistant to such a face lift, arguing that the sags and wrinkles of the West Village are precisely what makes it so charming, but capitalism won out.

*It's come a long way in recent years, but the Meatpacking District hasn't totally lost touch with the past.*

The West Village runs right into its northern neighbor – the unromantically-named Meatpacking District. Though this doesn't sound like it would offer much beyond cow parts, it's the latest hip area with a new Apple store to confirm its arrived. It began with a few good restaurants, created to serve locals and lure others down for dinner. Now people are coming for an off-the-beaten-path experience that goes beyond your standard fare of clothes, furniture, and gift stores.

## Christopher Street

Christopher Street, running through the heart of the West Village, has become synonymous with gay culture, and is lined with stores with names like 'The Pleasure Chest' and 'The Exotic Boutique,' selling products to live up to those names. There are an equal number of costume-type shops, appropriate since this neighborhood is host to New York's frenetic Halloween Parade. More than shops, cafés and sex and bondage toys, though, Christopher Street really offers a sampling of flamboyancy and community – both of which are qualities of gay culture.

### LOCAL ATTRACTIONS

Because the West Village is one of the oldest residential neighborhoods in New York, the houses and **quaint little streets** are an attraction in and of themselves. If you make it all the way west to the river, it's a beautiful walk, or cycle, along the newly renovated **esplanade** that runs along the Hudson from 23rd Street south to Battery Park City, with more renovations planned. The intersection of Christopher Street, Waverly Place, and Seventh Avenue is home to the famous 1969 Stonewall Riots, also known as the gay uprising. The Jefferson Branch of the **New York Public Library** is one of the most beautiful branches and, as a bonus, has the **Jefferson Garden**.

# Fashion & Footwear

### Andy's Chee-Pees
*18 West 8th Street [B2].*
*Tel: (212) 420-5980.*
The vintage or antique clothes here, from old camp T-shirts to Bowling League jackets, have long been outfitting hip New Yorkers.

### French Connection
*700 Broadway [C2].*
*Tel: (212) 473-4486.*
*www.frenchconnection.com*
The British French Connection chain, specializing in street-wise styles for 20- and 30-somethings, revamped its style through its FCUK ad campaign. Their many shops in New York got a face lift to accentuate this hip new look. BRANCHES: 1270 Sixth Avenue, Midtown; 435 West Broadway.

### James Perse
*411 Bleecker Street [A2].*
*Tel: (212) 620-9991.*
*www.jamesperse.com*
Comfy, casual clothing for men and women – most styles stay constant from year to year and are great basics, since most come in solid colors. Though it might seem absurd to pay $100 for a T-shirt, they are made to last.

### Jussara Lee
*11 Little West 12th Street [C1].*
*Tel: (212) 242-4128.*
Not only does this shop make items to fit each individual's size exactly, it also offers a service by which customers' own designs are made up into garments. Most of the designs are straightforward – such as light wool pants, leather skirts, and linen dresses – but they can have features added to make them more individual.

### Laina Jane Lingerie
*45 Christopher Street [B2].*
*Tel: (212) 807-8077.*
There's nothing extra-special about this store, which carries a variety of lingerie designers, but it's a friendly place with staff who can help you find something sexy, or practical.
BRANCH: 416 Amsterdam Avenue, Upper West Side.

### La Petite Coquette
*51 University Place [C1].*
*Tel: (212) 473-2478.*
This saucily named shop – it means 'little flirt' – does great lingerie, from the everyday to the totally seductive. It's a popular place for men to shop for gifts.

### Marc Jacobs
*403–5 Bleecker Street [A2].*
*Tel: (212) 924-0026.*
*www.marcjacobs.com*
This shop carries Marc Jacobs' line of casual separates, shoes, and accessories. Lines are classic, fabrics luxurious, and prices as steep as you would expect for a big-name designer. The presence of this high-end store ushered in a dozen other brand-name boutiques to the area.

### Purdy Girl
*540 La Guardia Place [C2].*
*Tel: (646) 654-6751.*
*www.purdygirlnyc.com*

**TIP**
The stretch of 8th Street from Sixth Avenue to Broadway is known as 'the shoe street.' The variety of shoe shops could be greater than it is, but there is still a decent range of affordable shoes to choose from.

*Brighten up at Bigelow's.*

*Bleecker is one of The Village's best known streets.*

The assortment of informal clothes goes from affordable to expensive, and includes items by a variety of designers, both well known and emerging.
BRANCH: 220 Thompson Street, Greenwich Village.

**Urban Outfitters**
*628 Broadway [C3].*
*Tel: (212) 475-0009.*
*www.urbanoutfitters.com*
Usually packed with teenage girls searching for this season's urban fashions, make-up, accessories, and other random 'must-have' items.
BRANCHES: across Manhattan.

## Jewelry & Accessories

**Gallery Eclectic**
*43 Greenwich Avenue [B1].*
*Tel: (212) 924-4314.*
*www.galleryeclectic.com*
Gallery Eclectic carries jewelry by local designers such as Catherine Angiel, and is popular with couples shopping for wedding and engagement rings.

## Health & Beauty

**C.O. Bigelow Apothecaries**
*414 Sixth Avenue [B2].*
*Tel: (212) 533-2700.*
*www.bigelowchemists.com*
An advertisement for this legendary drugstore reads: 'If you

can't get it anywhere else, try Bigelows,' and this couldn't be more appropriate – they stock everything from homeopathic remedies to imported toothpaste, with the added appeal of shopping in an old-time drugstore.

**L'Occitane en Provence**
*247 Bleecker Street [B2].*
*Tel: (212) 367-8428.*
*www.loccitane.com*
Beautifully packaged bath and beauty products with fragrances reminiscent of the South of France. Bags are made from seaweed, no products are tested on animals, and products are also labeled in Braille. Their sister store, Oliviers & Co., located next door, has a variety of olive oils, and other products with olive oil as their vital ingredient.
BRANCHES: across Manhattan.

## Design & Interiors

**Broadway Panhandler**
*65 East 8th Street [C2].*
*Tel: (866) 266-5927.*
*www.broadwaypanhandler.com*
Cutlery and cookbooks, pots and potholders, pepper grinders, electric mixers, pastry-cutters, chef's knives... you name it, this vast kitchen supply store will stock it, and all at highly affordable prices. This is *the* place to kit out your kitchen.

**Did you know?**
New York's famous Halloween Parade makes its way up Sixth Avenue through Greenwich Village. If you're not in costume, you'll definitely stand out. Don't worry, though, because there are a number of stores in the neighborhood where you can pick up a wig – try Ricky's, at 590 Broadway – and other fuss-free fancy-dress items.

*Lighting Plus and Hable Construction, two shops to transform your home.*

### Hable Construction
*117 Perry Street [A2].*
*Tel: (212) 989-2375.*
*www.hableconstruction.com*
Heavy duty canvas covered in bright, cheery colors – the products that this store carries are both decorative – floor pillows, blankets – and practical – gardening gloves, under the bed storage, pencil cases.
BRANCHES: across Manhattan.

### Lighting Plus
*680 Broadway [C2]*
*Tel: (212) 979-2000*
This store has an enormous range of lights, from floor lamps, hanging lamps, and table lamps for everyday use, to strings of lights for the garden, Chinese lanterns, Christmas lights, and much, much more.

### Mxyplyzyk
*125 Greenwich Avenue [A1].*
*Tel: (212) 989-5094.*
Though impossible to pronounce, this quaint little shop specializes in decorative home items and gift ideas. The owners take pride in what they sell – from laundry baskets to dinnerware and candles.

## Books & Music

### Biography Bookshop
*400 Bleecker Street [A2].*
*Tel: (212) 807-8655.*
If you are looking for an obscure biography, this small independent store is a great place to search beyond the bestsellers. The shop also carries other genres, and the staff are helpful and well informed.

### Bleecker Street Records
*239 Bleecker Street [B2].*
*Tel: (212) 255-7899.*
*www.bleeckerstreetrecords.com*
Rock, jazz, alternative, and much more – new and used – are available at this Bleecker Street store. The very knowledgeable staff are a great help, although they might be a little scornful if you ask for the new Madonna CD.

### Global News Inc.
*22 Eighth Avenue [A1].*
*Tel: (212) 645-1197.*
Global News stocks magazines for every interest, from fetish to niche adventure sports and local and world news.

### Partners & Crime
### Mystery Booksellers
*44 Greenwich Avenue [B1].*
*Tel: (212) 243-0440.*
*www.crimepays.com*
A huge selection of crime and mystery books – if you have a mystery fanatic in your life, this makes a great gift shop.

### Shakespeare & Company
*716 Broadway [C2]. Tel: (212) 529-1330. www.shakeandco.com*
The Hollywood movie 'You've Got Mail' was based on the story of the

Shakespeare store that had existed on the Upper West Side for years, and was put out of business when book superstore Barnes & Noble moved in next door. Luckily this branch stayed in business.
BRANCHES: across Manhattan. Tel: above number for details.

**Strand Bookstore**
*828 Broadway [C1]. Tel: (212) 473-1452. www.strandbooks.com*
This is Umberto Eco's 'favorite place in America,' and Steven Spielberg gave the shop $30,000 to furnish him with a 4,000-title library. The cavernous, disheveled, family-run store has 2½ million books from half-price review copies to $100,000 rarities. Born in 1927, it's an institution.
BRANCH: 95 Fulton St, Downtown.

## Gifts & Souvenirs

**Alphaville**
*226 West Houston Street [B3]. Tel: (212) 675-6850. www.alphaville.com*
The quirky items on sale at this West Village fixture – from old lunch boxes to obscure vinyl albums – wouldn't look out of place at a garage sale. However, the quality is generally pretty decent.

**Fassbinder**
*39 Eighth Avenue [A1] Tel: (212) 206-3600*
The eclectic items sold at Fassbinder, from ashtrays to

martini shakers, might best be described as *objets d'art*. Many of the designs are Art Deco influenced – often replicas of original designs with a contemporary twist.

## Children

**City Cricket**
*555 Hudson Street [A2]. Tel: (212) 242-2258. www.citycricket.com*
Children's clothes galore. This West Village favorite has a kid-friendly environment that caters to the locals with trendy clothes. They also sell furniture and kid's items.

**Estella**
*493 Sixth Avenue [B1]. Tel: (212) 255-3553. www.estella-nyc.com*
Estella stocks baby clothes from designers who also do adultwear – from Three Dots, Antik Batik, and Judith Lacroix, among others. The majority of the gorgeous baby designerwear sold here is exclusive to this store.

**Geppetto's Toy Box**
*10 Christopher Street [B2]. Tel: (212) 620-7511. www.nyctoys.com*
This supremely child-friendly store on Christopher Street stocks a full range of toys for all ages.

**Lucky Wang**
*799 Broadway [C1]. Tel: (212) 353-2850.*
A children's boutique catering

*All American peanut butter in 21 different varieties at this Sullivan Street novelty.*

*Long games and take-out refreshment at the Village Chess Shop.*

mostly to infants and toddlers. In addition to carrying their own line of clothing, which can be purchased at other stores, they also carry a handful of other designers. The Seventh Avenue store has a bigger selection.
BRANCH: 82 Seventh Avenue.

### Yoya
*636 Hudson Street [A1].*
*Tel: (646) 336-6844.*
*www.yoyashop.com*
Irresistible clothes for trendy tots by Petit Bateau and Judith Lacoix. Furniture is carried here too, including David Netto.
BRANCH: **Yoyamart**, 15 Gransevoort Street, West Village.

## Food & Drink

### Balducci's
*81 Eighth Avenue [A1].*
*Tel: (212) 741-3700.*
*www.balduccis.com*
At one time, Balducci's was New York's premier fancy food store, now it is one of a dozen, but it's still special and has a few surprises.
BRANCH: 155 A West 66th Street.

### Chocolate Bar
*48 Eighth Avenue [A1].*
*Tel: (212) 366-1541.*
*www.chocolatebarnyc.com*
Stop here to sample the delicious homemade chocolates, or buy a box for the road.

### is-wine
*24 West 8th Street [C2].*
*Tel:(212) 254-7800.*
An innovative wine merchants with tastings on Saturdays (4–7pm).

### Peanut Butter & Co.
*240 Sullivan Street [C2].*
*Tel: (212) 677-3995.*
*www.ilovepeanutbutter.com*
This shop does everything for Peanut Butter lovers – or for those obsessed. Stocks 21 varieties of the sticky nutty paste.

### Murray's Cheese Shop
*254 Bleecker Street [B2].*
*Tel: (212) 243-3289.*
*www.murrayscheese.com*
A favorite for New Yorkers and visitors alike, and what keeps them coming is not only the range and quality, but the good old-fashioned service. Now you can buy more than cheese and even take one of their cheese-related classes.

## Specialist

### Fetch
*43 Greenwich Avenue [B1].*
*Tel: (212) 352-8591.*
*www.caninestyles.com*
A department store for your pet pooch or cat, Fetch stocks every-

thing from dog beds and collars to cat-carrying cases.

## Flight 001

*96 Greenwich Avenue [B1].*
*Tel: (212) 691-1001.*
*www.flight001.com*
Wherever you're going, Flight 001 should have relevant guidebooks and maps, and handy products, including nylon travel bags, blow-up pillows, and first-aid kits.

## The Ink Pad

*22 Eighth Avenue [A1].*
*Tel: (212) 463-9876.*
*www.theinkpadnyc.com*
Has the city's largest range of ink pads and ink stamps. You can even create your own design.

## The Original Firestore

*17 Greenwich Avenue [B2].*
*Tel: (800) 229-9258.*
Memorabilia, toys, and sportswear from the New York Police and Fire departments. Unsurprisingly, their

popularity has grown following the heroic efforts of September 11th.

## Verve

*353 Bleecker Street [A2].*
*Tel: (212) 691-6516.*
Bags, belts, and wallets carefully selected by the owners, who only carry one or two unique items by a single designer.

## Village Chess Shop

*230 Thompson Street [C2].*
*Tel: (212) 475-9580.*
*www.chess-shop.com*
This chess fanatics' shop is open seven days a week, from 11am to midnight. It's always jam-packed with chess junkies entrenched in hours-long games.

## Village Paper Party Store

*18 Greenwich Avenue [B2].*
*Tel: (212) 675-9697.*
Whether you want kitsch or conventional, this fun store caters to all of your party needs.

## WHERE TO UNWIND

### Florent

*69 Gansevoort Street [A1]*
*Tel: (212) 989-5779*
Florent was here long before the Meatpacking District became fashionable. It's open almost 24 hours on weekdays (9am–5am) and all night on the weekends. The dinner menu is basic but relaxed, in line with the area's ambience.

### 'ino

*21 Bedford Street [B3]*
*Tel: (212) 989-5769*
Light bites including panini sandwiches and tapas of cheeses and olives can be enjoyed in this tiny café/wine bar. Always seems to draw a crowd without being overly packed.

### The Magnolia Bakery

*401 Bleecker Street [A2]*
*Tel: (212) 462-2572*
This store feels just like grandma's kitchen, and the freshly packed goods are as good as

the ones grandma makes. Treats include peanut-butter pie, banana pudding with vanilla wafers, and their infamous cupcake corner.

### Tea & Sympathy

*108 Greenwich Avenue [A1]*
*Tel: (212) 807-8329*
Anglophiles will find this a great place to enjoy high tea in a cozy setting. You should feel right at home, and the delicious home-baked goods only enhance this feeling.

### Village Vanguard

*178 Seventh Avenue South [B1]*
*Tel: (212) 255-4037*
Greenwich Village has long been a destination for jazz artists, and there is still a plethora of jazz clubs to choose from in this neighborhood. The Village Vanguard is perhaps the most consistently good spot, drawing favorites such as Wynton Marsalis and Chucho Valdes.

# SOHO

*Artsy and surreal by turns, Soho serves up a smorgasbord of fashion, curios and bric-a-brac for hard-core shoppers*

**S**oho is hip and trendy. Its inhabitants wear all black and whatever is in season at all times, intimidating visitors in from the 'burbs. It was New York's first high-end, trendy neighborhood. What the Village was to the rebellious Sixties, Soho is to the excessive Noughties.

There's commerce here, too, with a whole lot of shopping going on, so naturally your top designers must have boutiques here. Other areas of New York have their attractions, like museums, history, and eating. Here it's shopping, with, of course, an arty flair. Most stores are likely to be open seven days a week. And though it is fashion central, the district is also home to almost every kind of store – purveyors of shoes, stationery, fragrances, furniture, and assorted goodies.

## Cute and Compact

The main drag around here is Houston Street, from which comes the name SoHo – **so**uth of **Ho**uston. And that's HOW-stun, by the way, not HEW-stun as in the Texas city of 'Houston, we have a problem' fame. The main boundaries are Sixth Avenue to the west, Lafayette to the east, Houston to the north and Canal to the south. As other shopping neighborhoods have popped up around Soho – there's Nolita to the east and Tribeca to the south – these delineations are taken all the more seriously. Like most of the rest of Manhattan, Soho is laid out on an easy-to-navigate grid plan, except that the streets actually have names instead of numbers. Most of the stores are packed into a relatively small area on attractive, sometimes cobblestoned streets, but there are also a few stores, mostly dealing with furniture and design, scattered to the west of Sixth Avenue. This relatively compact area is well supplied with a large number of stores, which makes for easy wandering, and although things thin out south of Broome Street and east of Broadway, this doesn't mean you shouldn't give these areas your attention as well, depending on time available. Some of the really unique stuff can be off the beaten path, especially if you're looking for such items as discounted perfumes, faux designer bags, umbrellas or Chinese herbs, all of which are offered around the intersection of Canal and Lafayette, where Soho begins to blur with Chinatown.

*Opposite: Ubiquitous fire escapes.*
*Below: Soho is style central.*

You can easily spend a good full day shopping in Soho, as long as the crowds and prices don't turn you off. And when all of the shoppers have gone home, the area has lots of restaurants and bars so there are reasons to come even when the shops have closed. As shop owners take advantage of these nighttime visitors, stores tend to stay open to 7pm or so, even later on Thursdays. Conversely, most don't open until 11 am, so you don't necessarily have to make this your first stop of the da

## Sweet Smell of Success

Soho has become synonymous with high-end fashion, characterized mostly by shops selling shoes, handbags, and clothing. For the most part the shops here are expensive, but the presence of Old Navy and H&M and the string of non-descript stores that line Broadway from Spring to Canal mean that you can find cheaper items as well. The gentrification of the area has led to some of the highest priced real estate in all of New York, forcing many of the artists who formerly lived here to head over to Brooklyn (which interestingly enough is currently undergoing its own residential/retail transformation; as go the artists, so goes the shopping.) The high rents have also forced the art galleries, which used to make up a good percentage of the storefronts, to move on to West Chelsea, Brooklyn, and Long Island City. There are still a few left, and all welcome visitors, but if you want to make a more serious visit and potential purchase, you should call for an appointment with one of the experts.

When Soho first made the transition to becoming a tourist attraction, it was the place to be for unique boutiques – fashion and furniture. Over the past few years most of these little boutiques have been taken over by top clothing designers – Michael Kors, Costume National, Marc Jacobs, Burberry, John Varvatos, La Perla, Louis Vuitton – who also sell their wares at the department stores and at their Upper East Side or Midtown flagship locations. These stores have a greater selection of these designers' collections, but in terms of actually making purchases, it's often best to head to the department stores, as they have better return policies and good sales *(see Tip on page 22)*. A few years ago Soho got its own major department store when Bloomingdale's opened on Broadway.

## Cruising Around

Chain stores are practically required to have a Soho location, which means that much of the area, especially down Broadway and West Broadway –

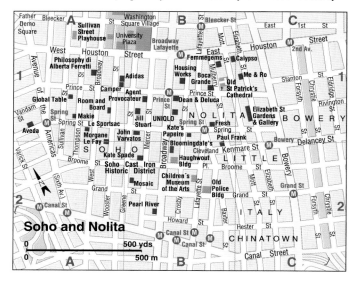

Soho and Nolita

where you'll find Banana Republic, Zara, Old Navy, and Nine West, among others – adds up to the equivalent of a glamorized outdoor mall. The Soho branch locations often offer some of the largest selections, but fighting the crowds means that it might be better to prioritize these shops in another neighborhood. You can find these stores in most other parts of Manhattan, so better to focus your time here on the high-end boutiques which are unique to this area.

*Above left: Famous Fanelli's*
*Above: Soho and high-end fashion go arm in arm.*

If you read fashion magazines or pay attention to what celebrities are wearing, the store names in Soho will immediately jump out at you – Prada, Armani, Channel, AG, Vivienne Westwood, plus all of those mentioned earlier. Because these high-end designers have practically become household names, they haven't been automatically listed in this chapter, unless, of course, the shop itself merits a visit or it provides a larger than usual collection of the designer. Given Soho's concentration of stores, it is simply impossible to go about naming them all. Most stores mentioned in the listings are still unique to New York or to Soho, or offer things that just shouldn't be missed.

## So Much to Buy

Though fashion seems to be Soho's priority, it also has some of the best furniture and design stores in the city. There's a range of goods – from modern designs to antiques to Asian or otherwise ethnic influenced – and a range of prices to match, though most fall into the higher than average price bracket, and some of the collections themselves look more like works of art than anything that could be considered functional or practical.

## LOCAL ATTRACTIONS

Though most else in New York City is changing at a rapid pace, **Canal Street** seems to stay the same. Vendors are packed tightly selling everything from perfume to fake Gucci bags and $5 pashminas. This is also the place to pick up souvenirs – postcards, replicas of the Statue of Liberty, New York Yankee t-shirts. The street is hectic with the pedestrian traffic, but Canal Street is also at the crossroads of many neighborhoods – TriBeCa, SoHo, NoLiTa and all roads lead to Chinatown; off of Canal Street are some amazing dim sum restaurants. The rest of the city will feel sleepy after this chaos.

*Prada exhibits its wares in the museum-like premises on Broadway.*

# Department Stores

### Bloomingdale's
*504 Broadway [B2].*
*Tel: (212) 729-5900.*
Soho now has its very own department store. Known as Petite Bloomies, it's much smaller than its uptown mother store and has a more personal, boutiquey feel. The emphasis here is on local designers.

# Fashion & Footwear

### Adidas
*136 Wooster Street [A1]. Tel: (212) 673-0398. www.adidas.com*
This fancy sneaker brand turned full service athletic wear has two stores in close proximity. One for fashion and the other more exclusively athletic.
BRANCH: 610 Broadway.

### AG-Adriano Goldschmied
*111 Greene Street [B1]. Tel: (212) 680-0581. www.agjeans.com*
The fancy denim jeans, which are made for women, men, and children can be altered here for free and there is a larger range than you will find in department stores.

### Agent Provocateur
*133 Mercer Street [B1].*
*Tel: (212) 965-0229.*
*www.agentprovocateur.com*
Ultra-fancy lingerie for the adventurous at heart. Studded whips, satin underwear, and sheer night gowns – more tasteful than raunchy.

### Agnes B.
*103 Greene Street [B1].*
*Tel: (212) 925-4649.*
*www.agnesb.com*
This fashionable French label produces well made separates that are both classic and contemporary. Sizes are on the small side.
BRANCHES: 1063 Madison Avenue, Upper East Side; 13 East 16th Street, Flatiron.

### American Eagle
*575 Broadway [B1].*
*Tel: (212) 941-9785*
*www.ae.com.*
Reasonably priced all-American clothing for the whole family.

### Anna Sui
*113 Greene Street [B1].*
*Tel: (212) 941-8406.*
Chinese-American designer Anna Sui finds inspiration in sharp 1950s cuts, '60s psychedelia and '70s glam rock. Try her crocheted, floral, and black, hippy-punk creations.

### Camper
*125 Prince Street [A1]. Tel: (212) 358-1842. www.camper.com*
Spain's signature shoe designer has made a big hit in America. Casual and comfortable, and occasionally quirky shoes.

### Jaime Mascaró
*430 West Broadway [A1].*
*Tel: (212) 965-8910.*
*www.mascaro.com*
A vast array of funky designer footwear for men and women. Pick up a bargain at the 60 percent-off sales.

### Jill Stuart
*100 Greene Street [B1].*
*Tel: (212) 343-2300.*
*www.jillstuart.com*
High-end women's fashion all under the feminine but practical Jill Stuart label. There's a range of vintage designs downstairs.

### John Varvatos
*122 Spring Street [B1].*

*Tel: (212) 965-0700.*
*www.johnvarvatos.com*
This men's clothier creates
designs that are practical and
unique, from striped shirts and
leather shoes to blue-velvet suits
and sling-back sandals.

**Joseph**
*106 Greene Street [B1].*
*Tel: (212) 343-7071.*
The popularity of the London
label among New Yorkers justifies
this vast branch. Understated
styles in cottons, and silks – practical yet chic, if on the pricey side.
BRANCH: 816 Madison Avenue,
Upper East Side.

**Marni**
*161 Mercer Street [B1].*
*Tel: (212) 434-3912.*
A relative newcomer on the fash-
ion/celebrity scene, these upmarket
women's clothes hail from Italy.
They are often in the moment,
unique and asymmetrical with
unexpected colors and adornments.

**Morgane Le Fay**
*67 Wooster Street [A2].*
*Tel: (212) 219-7672.*
*www.morganelefay.com*
Layers of silk, chiffon, organza,
and other fine fabrics are used to
create the kind of wispy romantic
dresses that little girls dream of.
They also make wedding dresses
*(see page 36).*
BRANCH: 746 Madison Avenue,
Upper East Side.

**Philosophy di Alberta Ferretti**
*452 West Broadway [A1].*
*Tel: (212) 460-5500.*
*www.philosophy.com*
The (supposedly) cheaper label
from Italian women's clothes
designer, Alberta Ferretti. When
everything else in Soho starts to
look alike, come here.

**Prada**
*575 Broadway [B1]. Tel: (212)*
*334-8888. www.prada.com*
Formerly the Guggenheim downtown, this wonderful space was
acquired and converted by Prada
to exhibit their high-end fashions.
Even if prices are out of reach, this
shop is a spectacle in itself.
BRANCHES: across Manhattan.

**Quiksilver**
*519 Broadway [B2].Tel: (212)*
*334-4500. www.quiksilver.com*
If you're a surfer, or want to look
like one, this place has the gear.
Bathing suits, mini skirts, boards,
watches, and canvas wallets.

**R by 45rpm**
*169 Mercer Street [B1]. Tel: (917)*
*237-0045. www.rby45rpm.com*
'R' is a clothing line from 45rpm,
a Japanese firm that specializes in
casual clothes based on American
styles of the 1950s and '60s. The
fashions are displayed amid
bamboo and waterfalls.

**Ted Baker**
*107 Grand Street [B2]. Tel: (212)*
*343-8989. www.tedbaker.com*

*Merchandise*
*from American-*
*inspired*
*Japanese store*
*R by 45rpm.*

*Listings*

*Kate Spade, a quintessential Soho store.*

This British fashion house has made a home in the States. Men's and women's fashions made trendy and made to last.

### UNIQLO
*546 Broadway [B1]. Tel: (212) 237-8800. www.uniqlo.com*
Cheap cashmere in a rainbow of colors is the staple of this addition to New York. Three floors of fashions for men, women and children complement the cashmere.

### Vivienne Tam
*40 Mercer Street [B2]. Tel: (212) 966-2398. www.viviennetam.com*
The title of her photo fashion book *China Chic* is also a succinct description of Vivienne Tam's East-meets-West designs.

## Jewelry & Accessories

### Anya Hindmarch
*115 Greene Street [B1].*
*Tel: (212) 343-8147.*
*www.anyahindmarch.com*
London designer Anya Hindmarch is famed for her unmistakable handbags, in particular her playful creations using photographs. Her latest idea is a canvas satchel that reads 'I'm not a plastic bag.'
BRANCH: 29 East 60th Street, Upper East Side.

### The Hat Shop
*120 Thompson Street [A1].*
*Tel: (212) 219-1445.*
*www.thehatshopnyc.com*
When Hollywood needs hats, they call The Hat Shop. Countless designs and colors on offer.

### Jill Platner
*113 Crosby Street [B1].*
*Tel: (212) 324-1298.*
*www.jillplatner.com*
This silver designer's studio is downstairs from the store, so you are guaranteed that the rings, belt buckles, and other body art are not being mass produced elsewhere.

### Kate Spade
*454 Broome Street [B2].*
*Tel: (212) 274-1991.*
*www.katespade.com*
Kate Spade's terminally hip handbags share her boutique with funky shoes, sunglasses, and other accessories. Her husband and business partner has opened a neighboring store for men.
*(Jack Spade, 56 Greene Street, tel: (212) 625-1820.)*
BRANCH: 135 Fifth Avenue, Flatiron.

### Le Sportsac
*176 Spring Street [A1]. Tel: (212) 625-2626.www.lesportsac.com*
The nylon handbag and luggage manufacturer has made a recent comeback. The firm keeps up with the fierce competition by matching their handbags to current trends.
BRANCH: 1065 Madison Avenue, Upper East Side.

## Oliver Peoples

*366 West Broadway [A2].*
*Tel: (212) 925-5400.*
*www.oliverpeoples.com*
There are a good half dozen sunglass and eyeglass stores scattered around Soho. If you're a sunglass junkie, Oliver Peoples always has an attractive collection, and the pod-like store is nice to browse in.
BRANCH: 755 Madison Avenue, Upper East Side.

## Reinstein/Ross

*122 Prince Street [A1]. Tel: (212) 226-4513. www.reinsteinross.com*
These elegant high carat gold and Indian gem designs are sought after. Such success breeds imitations and jewelry shoppers will doubtless spot copies for a fraction of the price, though nothing beats the understated elegance of an original.
BRANCH: 29 East 73rd Street, Upper East Side.

# Health & Beauty

## Aveda

*233 Spring Street [A1]. Tel: (212) 807-1492. www.aveda.com*
All of Aveda's deliciously scented skin- and bodycare products are made with natural plant and flower extracts, and none is tested on animals. This is also a beauty salon, but you'll need to book.
BRANCHES: across Manhattan.

## MAC

*113 Spring Street [B1].*
*Tel: (212) 334-4641.*
*www.maccosmetics.com*
Though most of the big department stores have a MAC counter, this huge branch of the Canadian cosmetics company offers a wider selection in a less chaotic environment, with experts on hand if you want a makeover.
BRANCH: 14 Christopher Street, West Village.

# Design & Interiors

## C.i.t.e

*131 Greene Street [B1].*
*Tel: (212) 431-7272.*
*www.citenyc.com*
This modern and industrial furniture and fixtures gallery is beyond modern for some and just right for those who want to live in the 21st century.

## Global Table

*107-109 Sullivan Street [A1].*
*Tel: (212) 431-5839.*
*www.globaltable.com*
The store is stuffed with treasures from around the world. Mostly tableware and decorative items: wooden bowls and delicate vases, for gifts and for you to take home.

## Michele Varian

*35 Crosby Street [B2].*
*Tel: (212) 343-0033.*
*www.michelevarian.com*
Big comfy floor cushions with throws to match, gorgeous pillows (paisley, striped, abstract, geometric), duvet covers and bedspreads to suit every taste and setting – all made on the premises by the designer herself. The store also displays other designers' work.

**TIP**
Because this neighborhood is packed with tourists, it's prime territory for pickpocketers. Keep your wallet in a secure place and stay away from the street games that are easy distractions. There are lots of plain-clothed police officers keeping watch, but they can't oversee everything.

*Colorful glassware at Michele Varian.*

### Mosaic: Antique & Contemporary Design
*49 Greene Street [B2].*
*Tel: (646) 613-8570.*
Much of Tribeca is devoted to furniture design and each store has its own very individual stamp. Mosaic's slant is decidedly ethnic, with etched wooden mirrors, decorative hand drums and low-set wooden stools.

### Pearl River
*437 Broadway [B2]. Tel: (212) 431-4770. www.pearlriver.com*
Items that you might otherwise find chaotically scattered around the shops of Chinatown have been neatly organized here. Though still reasonably priced, these Chinese lanterns, silk slippers, and tea pots are certainly more expensive, albeit better packaged, than what you will find blocks away.

### Room & Board
*105 Wooster Street [A1].*
*Tel: (212) 334-4343.*
*www.roomandboard.com*
If you are looking for mass-produced affordable furniture that looks more unique, Room & Board is where to come. This chain store hails from the Midwest and the styles have a wholesome appearance with a modern flair.

### Sur La Table
*75 Spring Street [B1]. Tel: (212) 966-3375. www.surlatable.com*
You can spend one dollar on a cookie cutter or hundreds on an expresso machine and everything in between. This store is similar to its rival Williams-Sonoma.

## Electronics

### The Apple Store
*103 Prince Street [B1]. Tel: (212) 226-3126. www.apple.com*
The Apple Store features every Apple product and accessory, as

well as running workshops and talks on maximizing your computer experience, from how to download music to how to edit movies.
BRANCHES: 767 Fifth Avenue, 401 West 14th Street.

## Books & Music

### Housing Works Used Book Café
*126 Crosby Street [B1].*
*Tel: (212) 334-3324.*
You can feel good about shopping here – whether you're buying a book or a latte in their café, proceeds go towards helping homeless New Yorkers living with Aids.

## Children

### Makie
*109 Thompson Street [A1].*
*Tel: (212) 625-3930.*
*www.makieclothier.com*
This pajama specialist also sells a sweet selection of hand-made children's clothes.

### The Scholastic Store
*557 Broadway [B1].*
*Tel: (212) 343-6166.*
The unprecedented success of the Harry Potter series probably gave this book publisher the market share (and money) it needed to turn the ground floor of its office building into a shop for its books, educational games and videos. They also do great programming and events for children.

## Food & Drink

### Dean & DeLuca
*560 Broadway [B1].*
*Tel: (212) 226-6800.*
*www.deananddeluca.com*
Stocks everything for the gourmet – those hard-to-find herbs and spices, chocolates, charcuterie, cheese, seafood, and foie gras, even

kitchenware – but quality comes at a price. There's also a coffee bar.
BRANCHES: across Manhattan.

*Novel footwear for indoors and out.*

# Specialist

### Bicycle Habitat
*244 Lafayette Street [B1].*
*Tel: (212) 431-3315.*
*www.bicyclehabitat.com*
According to *New York Magazine* this is 'New York's Best Bike Shop.' They specialize in building, selling, repairing, and renting a bikes and also organize bike rides.

### Eastern Mountain Sports (EMS)
*591 Broadway [B1]. Tel: (212) 966-8730. www.ems.com*
Eastern Mountain Sports stocks all the gear you might need for your next climbing, hiking, backpacking, or skiing adventure.

### Kate's Paperie
*72 Spring Street [B1].*
*Tel: (212) 941-9816.*
Reams of paper in all colors, sizes, and shapes. You'll also find a wide range of gift cards and wrapping.

## WHERE TO UNWIND

### Balthazar
*80 Spring Street [B1]*
*Tel: (212) 965-1785*
When this French bistro first opened, it took months to get a reservation, then Seinfeld got engaged here which made it even more popular. The restaurant and bar serve everything from snacks to full meals, and the adjacent patisserie is a welcome respite from the chaos of Soho. Dinner reservations essential.

### Bar 89
*89 Mercer Street [B1]*
*Tel: (212) 274-0989*
The signature feature of this trendy spot isn't its chocolate Martini (worth experiencing), but the bathroom doors, which fog up when latched – or more importantly don't fog up when not latched properly. User beware.

### Bliss Spa
*568 Broadway [B1]*
*Tel: (212) 219-8970*
This downtown spa became so popular that they had to open an uptown location to accommodate all of their clients. Choose from the à la carte menu of skin care and body care treatments, massages, waxing, manicures, and pedicures. All blissfully relaxing, but you'll need to book ahead and be prepared to flex the plastic.

### Fanelli's
*94 Prince Street [B1]*
*Tel: (212) 431-5744*
A long-established Soho fixture, Fanelli's started life as a speakeasy in the 1920s and remains a popular down-to-earth beer and burger joint. With its tiled floor and wooden bar, the pub has a cozy olde worlde feel that provides an escape from the relentless hipness of Soho. Open 'til late.

### Once Upon A Tart
*135 Sullivan Street [A1]*
*Tel: (212) 387-8869*
Two stores next to each other, one for takeout and one for sitting in. The menu is simple – basically sandwiches and pastries – but the orange ginger scones and hand-painted cookies take the simplicity and make it divine. Open until 8pm.

# Area 8: Nolita

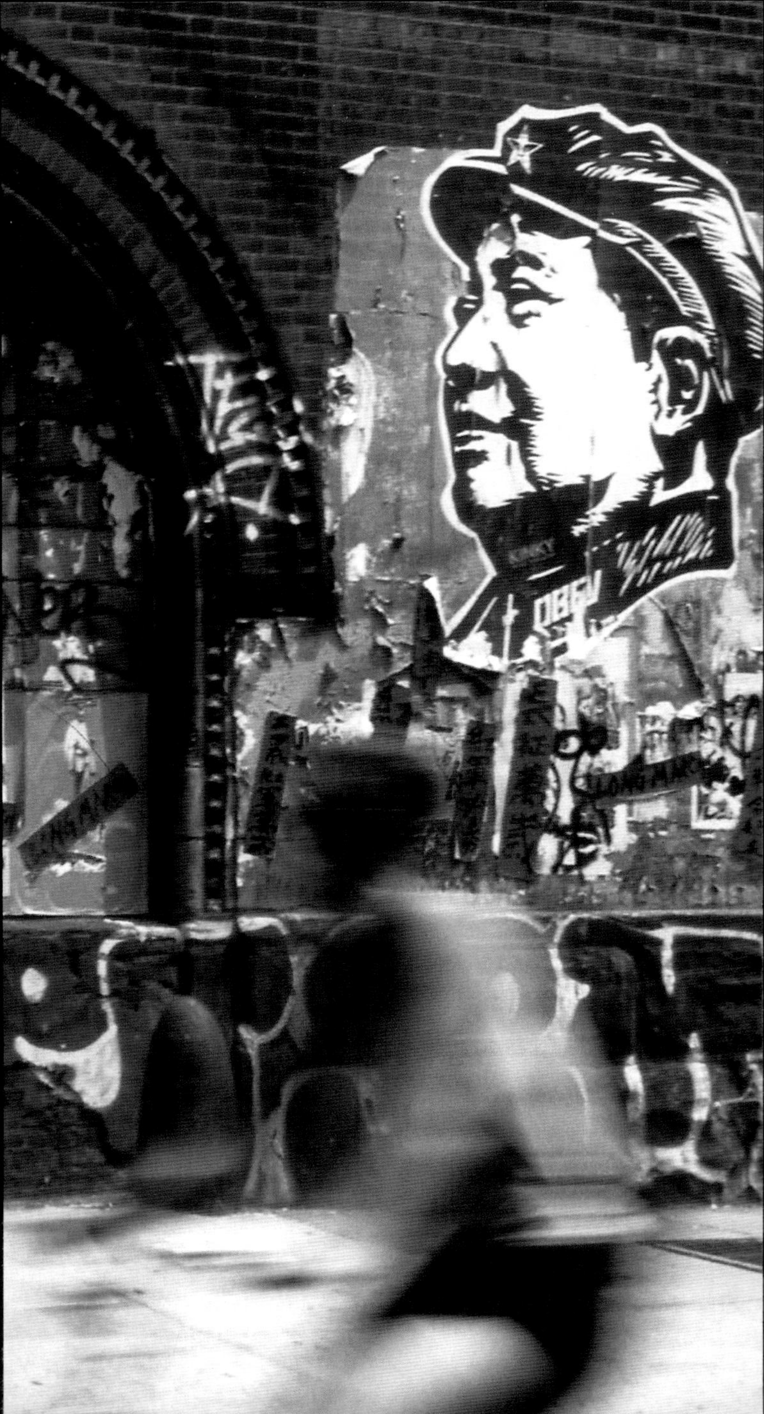

# NOLITA

*Even as a neighborhood inundated with fashionistas, it still manages to hold on to its authentic old world charm*

Map on page 82

**A**s neighborhoods go, Nolita is fairly new in the New York panorama, a pleasant combination of its eastern and western neighbors. To the west is Soho, which is beginning to spread its influence as it outgrows itself. To the east is the Lower East Side, which has the smaller boutiques that were once solely characteristic of Nolita. In a very short space of time, Nolita has grown from being a place for residents, mostly first- and second-generation immigrants from Italy and China, to being one of the hippest neighborhoods in this wonderfully diverse town. True to its roots, it draws a European crowd and its sights and smells are reminiscent of many a small town in Europe.

The stores in Nolita attract people on the hunt for something more unusual, but who perhaps aren't sufficiently dedicated in their search to bother venturing over to the East Village or Brooklyn (both equally good areas for unique buys). Prices in many cases remain uninflated, though the number of expensive designer boutiques, gift shops, and jewelers is on the increase. These are a magnet for fashionistas who can afford to spend $400 on a pair of pants without a second thought.

## Blending Old and New

You can call it Nolita or you can call it NoLita or you can call it NoLiTa. It's another one of those acronymic inventions, with a Nabokovian twist. It abbreviates **No**rth of **Li**ttle **Ita**ly, covering the three- to four-block area south of Houston Street. The focus of the neighborhood is three main streets – Mulberry, Mott, and Elizabeth; it is bounded by Lafayette to the west, where it immediately becomes Soho, and the Bowery to the east, where the Lower East Side begins. South of Spring Street, shops are a bit more sparse, but keep walking and you'll soon hit Chinatown and Little Italy, which offer herbal medicine stores, Italian bakeries, and other ethnic eateries, including plenty of dim sum palaces, as well as other specialty shops *(see page 99 for more on ethnic shopping in this area)*.

Although Nolita is residential as much as it is commercial, many people wandering the streets seem to be tourists, or at least visitors from other parts of New York. One appealing aspect of the area is that it hasn't been entirely overtaken by a professional class, so next to the trendy stores that line Elizabeth and Mott Streets is the hardware store that has been there for decades, along with Moes Meat Market, which no longer sells meat, but has preserved their storefront. In the summer, you're also likely to see old-timers sitting on folding lawn chairs in front of their apartments. It's a good mix of the old ways of lower Manhattan, once home to waves of immigrants, and new phenomena – yuppies spending their hefty bonuses, for example.

The stores themselves have mostly kept their original facades and architecture as they found them, which makes it easy to assume that they're either someone's private property or just a

*Opposite: Chinatown mural. Below: Alternative décor at Erica Tanov.*

*Right: Summer heat in Little Italy. Far right: Restaurant in Chinatown.*

small local store, and walk on by. Only a decade ago, few of the high-end stores existed, and most stores functioned to meet the needs of the local residents. This part of New York has traditionally been an immigrant area, and is still home to a few remaining sweatshops. Hidden behind some of these fancy shops are rooms packed with mostly Asian women working on sewing machines and making less than $1 an hour.

## A Shopping Community

Nolita is one of the smallest areas covered in this guide, but is deserving of its own chapter because the district provides some quite distinctive shopping opportunities. Together with the East Village and the Lower East Side, it is one of the last places in Manhattan where you can still make real 'finds,' and discover small boutiques and other shops off the beaten path that are unknown outside of New York.

The upside to these shops is that you're able to get unique items whose prices haven't been overinflated. The downside is that many of the independent local designers are still making a go of it, which means there's a risk they won't be able to afford to stick around once their three-year leases have run out. The current challenged economy makes this all the more likely.

Many of these boutiques are run by the designers and owners themselves, who are often on hand to make simple alterations, suggestions, or to give you some background on their approach to design or business philosophy. Their workshops and studios are usually in the back of the store, so the claim 'locally made' is, for once, absolutely genuine. The majority of these designers are young women who are first-time business owners. There is a strong community spirit here, and most boutique owners are supportive of their neighbors – a refreshing change from the usual competitive nature of shopkeepers.

Nolita remains resistant to the infiltration of trendy, expensive stores, but as Soho grows it is encroaching on Nolita's territory. Tory Burch's uber-preppy designs and Sigerson Morrison shoes look as if they belong more in Soho than in Nolita, but these stores are still in the minority and hopefully the neighborhood can hang on to its appealingly individual character.

The creativity of its homegrown designers makes Nolita a potential victim of their success. Local pioneers such as Me & Ro and Mayle now have their jewelry and clothing sold at the leading department stores, where they command top prices. Although local resistance to total gentrification remains strong, prices are forcing neighboring designers to compete or disappear.

## Specialty Shops

Women's clothing stores dominate Nolita, but tucked in between the parade of boutiques that draw fashionistas like a magnet, you'll find a remarkable number of specialty shops. Dinky little stores devoted solely to lighting, mix-and-match bikinis, lingerie, handbags, glasses, stone and marble carvings, hand-tooled boots, that you can easily dip in and out of.

Along the Bowery, the eastern edge of Nolita, is a concentration of kitchen supply and lighting stores. Further east begins the world of wholesale fabrics; to the south are specialty hardware stores. They cater to wholesalers, but are quite willing to sell to the general public. This is the place to find the greatest range and often the best prices. Also here you'll find popcorn stands, hot dog grills and other things the average homeowner can probably manage without.

## Hanging Out

One of the most pleasant districts to stroll around, Nolita is also one of the best places to sit and watch the world go by. There is a wide range of coffee bars, restaurants and cafes – cosy and homey, quirky or chichi, the majority have an enjoyably local flavor.

## Fashion & Footwear

### Baby Blue Line

*238 Mott Street [B1].*
*Tel: (212) 226-5866.*
A small collection of simple but youthful women's separates, from hand-printed dresses to casual tops, created by a Korean designer who owns and runs the boutique herself. Prices are reasonable for such well made clothes.

### Calypso

*280 Mott Street [B1]. Tel: (212)*
*965-0990. www.calypso-celle.com*
These tropically-colored women's clothes make a welcome change from the mandatory New York black. Other stores in the area include one for kids clothing and an outlet store – one ongoing sale.
BRANCHES: across Manhattan.

### Dö Kham

*51 Prince Street [B1].*
*Tel: (212) 966-2404.*
Exotic items from Tibet and the Himalayas, such as lightweight silk tops, sarongs in an array of colors, and wonderful brocaded silk hats.

### Erica Tanov

*204 Elizabeth Street [C1].*
*Tel: (212) 334-8020.*
*www.ericatanov.com*
Sophisticated womenswear is the main focus, with clothes by well known designers such as Piazza Sempione and Three Dots, as well as Tanov's own designs. There is also a kiddies' corner and a small selection of bed linens.

*The latest European styles at Otto Tootsi Plohound.*

## Henry Lehr & Co, Inc.
*9 Prince Street [C1].*
*Tel: (212) 274-9921.*
A huge stock of men's and women's jeans in a range of styles from various trendy labels, and casual tops to match.

## Ina
*21 Prince Street [C1]. Tel: (212)*
*334-9048. www.inanyc.com*
Ina is a resale shop and includes nearly new clothes – in perfect condition – by top designers. If you don't mind being one season out of fashion, all three locations offer some great finds.
BRANCHES: 208 East 73rd Street; 15 Bleecker Street.

## Malia Mills
*199 Mulberry Street [B1].*
*Tel: (212) 625-2311.*
*www.maliamills.com*
Sporty swimsuits and bikinis you can mix and match in a range of styles and colors. The store has a well-earned reputation for its ability to cater for all body shapes.
BRANCH: 220 Columbus Avenue and 1031 Lexington Avenue.

## Matta
*241 Lafayette Street [B1].*
*Tel: (212) 343-9399.*
*www.mattany.com*
Carefully chosen women's fashions – many with Matta's own label. Soft cotton skirts, colorful hand knits, and simple t-shirts, also accessories and kid's clothing.

## Mayle
*242 Elizabeth Street [C1]*
*Tel: (212) 625-0406*
Mayle's womenswear, now available around the world, started life here in this Nolita store. Highly individual, often whimsical women's clothing, plus a wide range of accessories.

## Mixona
*262 Mott Street [B1]. Tel: (646)*
*613-0100. www.mixona.com*

With so much lingerie, swim- and sleepwear in one room, this chic shop is bound to have something for everyone. All the best labels are stocked and styles range from simple, cotton bras to sexy silks and bright orange bathing suits.

## Otto Tootsi Plohound
*273 Lafayette Street [B1]*
*Tel: (212) 431-7299*
Men's and women's shoes, and plenty of variety. Mostly high-end imports (Prada, Gianfredi Fantini), but you can find good buys, especially in the sales, when prices are cut by up to 75 percent.
BRANCHES: 137 Fifth Avenue

## Paul Frank
*195 Mulberry Street [B2].*
*Tel: (212) 965-5079.*
*www.paulfrank.com*
Showroom for this pop designer. A distinct 1950s influence in the shapes and colors. Shirts, T-shirts, wallets, sunglasses, furniture, homewares, and a random assortment of gift items are available.

## Resurrection
*217 Mott Street [C1].*
*Tel: (212) 625-1374.*
*www.resurrectionvintage.com*
Even at these resale prices, a Pucci dress will set you back a fistful of dollars. The Harley Davidson T-shirts and Vans pumps are cheaper.

## Seize sur Vingt
*243 Elizabeth Street [C1].*
*Tel: (212) 343-0476.*
*www.16sur20.com*
Gwendolyn Jurney's own designs for men and women. Mostly pinstripe shirts and suits for the businessman or woman, but it's all a timeless, classic look – and most of the shirts require cufflinks.

## Shoe
*247 Mulberry Street [B2].*
*Tel: (212) 925-1735.*
*www.bagandshoe.com*
The name says it all, but this

no-fuss leather store in addition to offering a range of women's and men's shoes also carries simply designed handbags and belts.

### Sigerson Morrison

*28 Prince Street [C1].*
*Tel: (212) 219-3893.*
*www. sigersonmorrison.com*
Cleanly styled ladies shoes, the epitome of elegance, at a price. They have great colors and styles, and a big selection. Sigerson Morrison have a handbag store nearby at 242 Mott Street.
BRANCH: 987 Madison Avenue.

### Tory Burch

*257 Elizabeth Street [C1].*
*Tel: (212) 334-3000.*
*www.toryburch.com*
This swanky clothing designer's Palm Beach styles stand out at this downtown location. The most complete collection but you can find smaller collections at most department stores.

### Tracy Feith

*209 Mulberry Street [B1].*
*Tel: (212) 334-3097.*
The surfer-turned-designer has a range of sexy but versatile women's clothing in unusual fabrics. His wafty silk and chiffon dresses in tropical colors are highly covetable (though not designed for the fuller figure). His creations also include shoes, hats, jewelry, handbags ...... and surfboards.

### Unis

*226 Elizabeth Street [C1].*
*Tel: (212) 431-5533.*
Men's clothing for those who want to branch out from the khaki and collar shirt uniform. Fashionable while managing to stay classic.

## Jewelry & Accessories

### Blue Bag

*266 Elizabeth Street [C1].*
*Tel: (212) 966-8566.*

From tiny purses to big diaper bags, from fancy to everyday, this store can meet all your handbag needs. Annual sale in August.

### Boca Grande

*49 Prince Street [B1].*
*Tel: (212) 334-7350.*
*www.bocagrandefurnishings.com*
Jewelry from around the world. Though you're certainly paying more than you would in any of the countries represented, it doesn't feel overpriced. And the same goes for their furniture store.
BRANCH: 54 Greene Street.

### Femmegems

*280 Mulberry Street [B1].*
*Tel: (212) 625-1611.*
At Femmegems you can make your own jewelry or have something designed for you. The quality is great, and it's better value than buying something by a hip designer. You might even find your vocation.

### Hiponica

*238 Mott Street [B1].*
*Tel: (212) 966-4388.*
Handmade bags and purses, designed by the owner to be fun and functional. About a dozen different designs are carried at any given time, from leather bags that barely hold more than your wallet to large cotton bags perfect for trips to the beach. Each design comes in a range of colors. There is also a co-ordinated range of wallets.

### Me & Ro

*241 Elizabeth Street [C1].*
*Tel: (917) 237-9215.*
*www.meandrojewelry.com*
Colorful pendants, bangles, and baubles 'inspired by natural forms.' Cast in silver and gold, with clusters of precious and semi-precious stones all set by hand, these designs have a handcrafted Indian flavor. Me & Ro jewelry is now available in many

*Beautiful jewelry for sale in beautiful surroundings at Me & Ro.*

*Fun fluffy slippers by Nancy Koltes.*

department stores, but this is the home base. Worth stopping by just to admire their innovative floral window designs.

## Health & Beauty

### Fresh
*57 Spring Street [B1]. Tel: (212) 925-0099. www.fresh.com*
Started by a few Russians and now, at least partially, acquired by a mega-company (LVMH), these beauty products are lauded for their natural ingredients. There's an attempt to make each product be as pure or as true to one ingredient as possible.
BRANCHES: across Manhattan.

### Red Flower
*13 Prince Street [C1]. Tel: (212) 966-5301. www.redflower.com*
An emporium of beautiful scents, these candles, soaps, and lotions are as much about their fragrance as their beautiful display.

## Design & Interiors

### AREA iD
*262 Elizabeth Street [C1]. Tel: (212) 219-9903. www.areaid.com*
This modern furniture store is run by the knowledgeable Inda Davidsson, who can help you accessorize any room. Lamps, Andy Warhol lookalike prints and other things modern.

### Just Shades
*21 Spring Street [C1]. Tel: (212) 966-2757. www.justshadesny.com*
An entire store devoted to lamp-shades and a great place to find that perfect lighting design.

### Nancy Koltes
*31 Spring Street [B1]. Tel: (212) 219-2271. www.nancykoltes.com*
The main focus is Nancy Koltes bed linen collection, but the store also features antique Indian quilts, sleepwear, table linens, and a choice of sexy and comfortable ladies' slippers.

### The Red Threads
*190 Elizabeth Street [C1]. Tel: (212) 925-6519. www.theredthreads.com*
What began as a small time Lower East Side pillowcase maker has now expanded and added hand-made unique furniture to their interesting textiles offering.

## Books & Music

### McNally Robinson
*52 Prince Street [B1]. Tel: (212) 274-1160. www.mcnallyrobinsonnyc.com*
A good old-fashioned bookstore in a warm and inviting space. The displays are so appealing they make you want to curl up and start reading right away. There is an indoor cafe where you can read the many books and magazines in

**Did you know?**
For 10 days in September, Little Italy celebrates the Feast of San Gennaro, patron saint of Naples. The festivities are centered on Mulberry Street, which is lined with stalls laden with food and wine.

**TIP**
What Tribeca is to the A-list movie star set, Nolita is to the independent film scene. Hanging out at Café Habana or nearby Café Gitane you might be lucky enough to spot film stars Vincent Gallo or Chloë Sevigny.

stock and on weekends they do storytime for kids.

## Gifts & Souvenirs

### Daily 2.3.5.
*235 Elizabeth Street [C1].*
*Tel: (212) 334-9728.*
Everything you didn't realize you wanted you can get at this quirky store – yoyos, xylophones, birthday cards, candles that won't blow out, sweet smelling soaps, etc. It's all endless fun!

## Children

### Lilliput
*265 Lafayette Street [B1].*
*Tel: (212) 965-9567.*
Choc-full of kid's clothes by mainly European designers. It's not easy to just browse, but ask and you will find. They have a huge selection of kids' shoes and cater to kids beyond the toddler years.

## Food & Drink

### Lunettes et Chocolat
*25 Prince Street [C1].*
*Tel: (212) 925-8800.*
An unusual combination: try on a pair of funky red sunglasses while sampling hand-dipped chocolates.

## Specialist

### Polux
*248 Mott Street [B1].*
*Tel: (212) 219-9646.*
Amid the chaos of this small New York neighborhood, this quiet flower shop, where French is always spoken, is a nice escape.

## WHERE TO UNWIND

**Bread**
*20 Spring Street [C1]*
*Tel: (212) 334-1015*
Paninis served in a relaxing setting. As the neighborhood grows in popularity, tiny restaurants like this one grow more crowded.

**Café Habana**
*17 Prince Street [C1]*
*Tel: (212) 625-2001*
There's always a crowd at this popular restaurant, with an adjacent take-out joint, but the menu of tasty Mexican specialties (try the corn on the cob soaked in butter and chili powder) are worth the wait.

**Chibi's Bar**
*238 Mott Street [B1]*
*Tel: (212) 274-0054*
Stop off for some sake and exotic appetizers or go next door to the Kitchen Club for the full Euro-Japanese fusion menu.

**Lombardi's Pizza**
*32 Spring Street [B1]*
*Tel: (212) 941-7994*
Lombardi's boasts the oldest ovens in New York and is still one of the best places for good thin-crust pizza in the city. Their specialty topping is clams. As with most of the best eateries around here, be prepared to wait.

# Little Italy & Chinatown

*Two of New York's most colorful neighborhoods,*
*under threat and shrinking, but still very much alive*

As the number of New Yorkers seeking stylish apartments and places to shop increases, the neighborhoods that once served the diverse populations of Manhattan have diminished. Most have been pushed out to the outer boroughs, namely Brooklyn and Queens. Of these ethnic enclaves, Little Italy and Chinatown have always been, and remain, the most popular with tourists and New Yorkers alike. Though the Little Italy and Chinatown of today have certainly shrunk from 20 years ago, both remain a mainstay of lower Manhattan. In the heart of these neighborhoods, you feel as if you have somehow been transported to another country, or perhaps even a time in New York's history when ethnic communities weren't marginalized, but celebrated. Few of the signs are in English, residents often speak another language, and the products being sold are specialties of these given regions rather than American imitations. It's not uncommon to enter a store selling Italian pastries, religious relics, Chinese herbs or Peking duck and not find anyone who speaks English. It's a refreshing reminder that these things aren't, in fact, 'imports' but a confirmation of the disparate strands that make the United States, and specifically New York, so wonderfully diverse.

## Food and Bargains

The most obvious attraction offered by these neighborhoods is their food. The number of restaurants, and the markets that crowd the sidewalks every day of the week, can satisfy both gourmets and hungry shoppers looking for a change from the usual roadside hot dog vendor. If you have the patience for these outdoor markets, you're likely to get the same produce sold to you by Dean & Deluca for a fraction of the price, minus, of course, the packaging and air-conditioned comfort. The same goes for the stores that are crammed full of bowls,

chopsticks, steamers, lanterns, and other exotica generally available in the smaller boutiques of Soho, for about twice the price. The best way to approach shopping here is just to wander around. There are plenty of bargains to be had and half the fun is in making your own discoveries.

*Authentic food is a big part of the appeal of these areas.*

# TRIBECA & DOWNTOWN

*Commercial development is putting new life into some old and venerable neighborhoods at the southern tip of Manhattan*

The common denominator of these three sections of New York – Wall Street, the South Street Seaport, and Tribeca – is that they're situated down at Manhattan's southern tip. Otherwise, they're widely different neighborhoods, and in terms of shopping are quite divergent. In all, shopping seems more like an afterthought here: the area was mainly residential before it became the financial center of the city. In neither phase was it known for its shopping facilities, but once tourists started to arrive for tours of the New York Stock Exchange or Trinity Church on Wall Street, for boat rides at the Seaport, and for Tribeca's restaurants, the natural next step was to add shops to keep people here longer and give them a few ideas on how to spend their money. Commercial development continues at a steady pace, so each new visit is likely to introduce you to new stores.

The neighborhoods we know as the South Street Seaport and the Wall Street financial district are among New York's oldest, but in past years this area has become famous as the former site of the World Trade Center. In the wake of the terrorist attacks of September 11, 2001, businesses worked hard to stay afloat, but with the help of high-end residences and reduced rents, new businesses have been lured back to the area. An influx of new restaurants and the opening of The Drawing Center are also adding to this neighbourhoods appeal. Most of the stores around here are either tourist shops or chain stores. Though shopping may not be uppermost in the minds of most visitors to this area, it's worth noting that two of the best stores in New York are here – J&R, the electronics and appliance megastore, and Century 21, a great retail discount store, offering top designer wear at sharply reduced prices.

Unlike the majority of other neighborhoods, weekends are a good time to visit, when all the worker bees have fled to the suburbs or to their uptown apartments and the streets are fairly empty. However, if you want to experience the frenetic side of Wall Street as portrayed in the movies, a weekday trip might be more satisfying.

*Opposite and below: Pier 17 at South Street Seaport.*

## Orientation

Stores in these areas tend to be concentrated on Fulton and Nassau streets, both closed to traffic at certain times of the day, and the Seaport. Walking in between these different sections, you won't find a huge number of stores to wander around in. You will, however, find more service-focused stores – for instance, those offering cell phones, drugstores, shoe repairs, office supplies – all things catering to those who might need to pick up some supplies in their lunch hour.

The World Trade Center site rebuilding program is still in full swing, which creates a challenge when navigating your way around. The streets in this neigh-

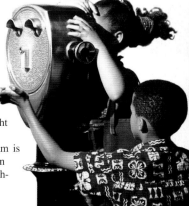

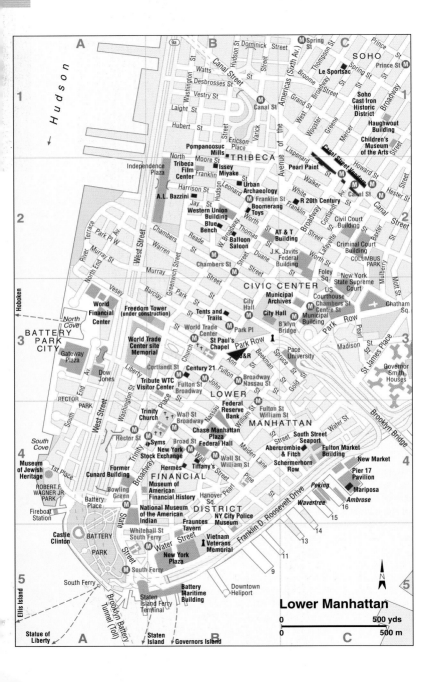

**Lower Manhattan**

| 0 | | 500 yds |
|---|---|---|
| 0 | | 500 m |

*Juice Bar in Tribeca.*

borhood, unlike those in much of the rest of Manhattan, aren't neatly organized into a grid system (a legacy of this being the earliest part of the city to be colonised); they run diagonally as much as on a north-south or east-west axis, and are named rather than numbered.

## Tribeca

The final piece of this triumvirate is Tribeca, which abbreviates **tri**angle **be**low **Ca**nal. Ten years ago this elite, mostly residential neighborhood contained only a few restaurants, antique furniture shops, and loft apartments. With the advent of converting loft spaces and onetime parking lots into fancy residential apartments, plus Robert De Niro's role as a restaurateur, this once sleepy area has been transformed into its own small town, home to some of New York's fanciest restaurants (Nobu, Bouley, Chanterelle) and expensive shopping of all kinds. In Duane Park, for instance, you'll find many exclusive furniture shops – some modern, some antique, but all expensive. Following 9/11, many of the high-end shops and restaurants, who depended heavily on the World Trade Center's pool of 100,000 workers, found it hard to stay afloat. Nowadays, there is a growing number of inexpensive and mid-range places on offer – something that makes it a very good time to visit Lower Manhattan, where now, more than ever, the customer rules.

### LOCAL ATTRACTIONS

This is a great neighborhood to wander around and absorb some of New York's history. Battery Park, at Manhattan's southern tip, is where you can catch ferries to the **Statue of Liberty** and **Ellis Island**. If you want to skip the tourist museums and just get out on the water, hop on the **Staten Island Ferry**.

Because this is Manhattan's oldest neighborhood it is also home to some of its great historic buildings, such as the U.S. Customs House, which now houses the **Museum of the American Indian**, **Trinity Church** and **St. Paul's Chapel**, and the **New York Stock Exchange**.

The grounds of the former World Trade Center are now a construction site, as work continues on Freedom Tower, a 1,776ft (541-meter) skyscraper to open in 2011. Visitors who would like a moment to reflect on the tragedy away from the sound of bulldozers are encouraged to go to **St Paul's Chapel.**

*Listings*

*Ann Taylor for the career woman.*

# Fashion & Footwear

## Abercrombie & Fitch
*199 Water Street [C4]. Tel: (212) 809-9000. www.abercrombie.com*
What used to be a shop for preppies is now on the wanted list of hip high schoolers who come here for their 'A & F' casuals. Loose-fitting shirts, knits, fleeces, denims, cargo pants, caps, etc. All practical, comfortable, and very American.
BRANCHES: across Manhattan.

## Ann Taylor
*4 Fulton Street [C4]. Tel: (212) 480-4100. www.anntaylor.com*
Ann Taylor has branches around Manhattan, all focused on outfitting the career woman with affordable suits and separates, weekend clothing, and evening wear. Ann Taylor Loft, also with several shops, has more casual and moderately priced lines. Well known for its sales.
BRANCHES: across Manhattan.

## Daffy's
*50 Broadway [B4]. Tel: (212) 422-4477. www.daffys.com*
'High fashion, low prices' is the tag line of this store, which mostly stocks men, women, and children's fashions, but also has a house wares section. Filled mostly with European designers – some top of the line, others you have never heard of. Come here for bargains, not necessarily for a unique shopping experience.
BRANCHES: across Manhattan.

## Express
*South Street Seaport, Pier 17, 1st Floor [C4]. Tel: (212) 693-0247. www.express.com*
Express is part of the Limited family, all of which offer moderately priced (and moderately made) up-to-the-minute clothing. Good solid colored pants and tops. If paired with a fancier label, no-one would

**Did you know**
Rarely will you have seen bodies this up close and personal. Less exploitative and more informative, this exhibit, simply titled Bodies, is an interesting and detailed exploration of our bodies. What was once the realm of medical experts is being showcased and demystified for the general public. Bodies: The Exhibition, 11 Fulton Street; (646) 837-0300. Tickets are a must.

guess you only paid $20 for a pair of black pants.
BRANCHES: across Manhattan.

## Guess
*23–25 Fulton Street [C4]. Tel: (212) 385-0533. www.guess.com*
Made famous by their jeans, this company has broadened its repertoire to include a wide range of separates and signature accessories, keeping its finger firmly on the teen fashion pulse.
BRANCH: 537 Broadway, Soho.

## Hermès
*15 Broad Street [B4]. Tel: (212) 785-3030. www.hermes.com*
Known for their men's ties and ladies scarves, this Parisian store is a big hit with Americans. This new location is a sign that Wall Street is becoming a tourist and residential destination.
BRANCH: 691 Madison Avenue.

## Issey Miyake
*119 Hudson Street [B2]. Tel: (212) 226-0100. www.isseymiyake.com*
The first designer clothing store to make an appearance in Tribeca. Miyake's cutting edge designs appeal to fashionistas who want to turn heads. The seemingly low-key neighbors, who are trying to keep things local, might not wish for its

success, but bringing business to Tribeca is the goal for others. BRANCH: 992 Madison Avenue, Upper East Side; **Pleats Please**, 128 Wooster Street, Soho.

### Syms
*42 Trinity Place [A4]. Tel: (212) 317-8200.*
Syms' 'I'm An Educated Consumer,' shopping bag slogan is appropriate for the savvy male and female customers carrying away their discounted designer clothing.

### Talbots
*189–191 Front Street [C4]. Tel: (212) 425-0166. www.talbots.com*
Talbots specializes in well-priced classic cut women's clothes. Solid-colored cotton and wool sweaters, and linen and wool pants. They have two seasonal sales a year, when prices get slashed by up to 70 percent. BRANCHES: across Manhattan.

### Victoria's Secret
*19 Fulton Street [C4]. Tel: (212) 962-8122. www.victoriassecret.com*
This lingerie company's models and their quasi-pornographic catalogue are probably more famous than their line of affordable lingerie. Many people prefer to buy online rather than fight the in-store crowds and uber-pink decor. BRANCHES: across Manhattan.

### The World Financial Center
*Vesey & West Street [A3]. Tel: (212) 417-7000. www.worldfinancialcenter.com*
Renovated after September 11th, this financial headquarter has an indoor mall featuring dozens of shops and restaurants. The space is beautiful with water views and displays of contemporary art. Stores here include children's clothing, toys, men's and women's fashions and accessories.

## Jewelry & Accessories

### Claire's Accessories
*South Street Seaport, Pier 17, 2nd Floor [C4]. Tel: (212) 566-0193. www.claires.com*
Usually packed with teen girls checking out the huge range of earrings and hair accessories – all are affordable enough to spend your babysitting money on. BRANCHES: across Manhattan.

**TIP**
Although Tribeca is only blocks away from Soho, its streets are infinitely less crowded, even on weekends. Note that shops are closed on Mondays.

*Mannequins at Issey Miyake's Tribeca store.*

*Juke box from Urban Archaeology. Below: J&R sells every electronic item under the sun.*

**TIP**

There are lots of star-sightings to be had in Tribeca. Robert De Niro made this neighborhood popular by opening up some of New York's most trendy restaurants. Other stars, like Ed Burns, Will Smith and Jada Pinkett, and Billy Crystal, among others, are now De Niro's neighbors.

## Sunglass Hut & the Watch Station

*South Street Seaport, Pier 17, 1st Floor [C4]. Tel: (212) 587-3974. www.sunglasshut.com*
This chain store can be found in almost every neighborhood of New York City, and selections vary little from outlet to outlet, but they carry all the major brands, from Versace, Dolce & Gabbana, Prada, and Ralph Lauren sunglasses to Fossil, Diesel, and DKNY watches.
BRANCHES: across Manhattan. Check the website for details.

# Health & Beauty

### Bath & Body Works

*South Street Seaport, Pier 17, 1st Floor [C4]. Tel: (212) 349-1561. www.bathandbodyworks.com*
Created to compete with The Body Shop, which also has a branch here, the Bath & Body Works shops bear a close resemblance to those of their rival, as do their health and beauty products – bath balls, fruit-flavored soaps, loofa sponges *et al*.
BRANCHES: across Manhattan.

### Duane Reade

*95 Wall Street [B4]. Tel: (212) 363-5830. www.duanereade.com*
As you walk around New York, you will notice a 'Duane Reade' store in practically every neighborhood. This drugstore chain has bought up most others in the city. Chaotic, but cheap.
BRANCHES: across Manhattan.

# Department Stores

### Century 21

*22 Cortland Street [B3]. Tel: (212) 227-9092. www.C21stores.com*
All the fancy clothes that you might not otherwise be able to afford are crammed into this

discount department store. Men's and women's fashion, household goods, and beauty products. Take advantage of their 7.45am opening time to avoid the crowds.

# Design & Interiors

### Butter and Eggs
*27 Howard Street [B3].*
*Tel: (212) 676-0235.*
*www.butterandeggs.com*
There is more to this store than meets the eye. They have beautiful house wares displayed as well as a few pieces of furniture and decorative items. But they offer much more than what is on display, including consulting services for how to decorate and design.

### Pompanoosuc Mills
*124 Hudson Street [B1].*
*Tel: (212) 226-5960.*
*www.pompy.com*
Pompanoosuc Mills do hardwood furniture made in Vermont (hand-crafted to order) – both reason enough to guarantee a solid, long-lasting dresser, bed frame, or mirror. Made in Vermont seems like an odd sell in the midst of ultra-hip Tribeca, but these unique pieces of furniture continue to pull in the crowds.

### R 20th Century
*82 Franklin Street [C2].*
*Tel: (212) 343-7979.*
*www.r20thcentury.com*
Tribeca is littered with antique furniture stores. This one focuses on 20th century pieces, with designs ranging from wooden chaise longues to three legged chairs. Some are extremely expensive, but there are bargains to be had, too.

### Stella
*138 West Broadway [B2].*
*Tel: (212) 233-9610.*
An irresistible range of beautiful linens and home accessories. The luxurious linen and silk sheets and pillow cases, which come in a variety of sizes and patterns, seem far too good to sleep on. Bath robes, slippers, and fine bath products are also sold.

### Urban Archaeology
*143 Franklin Street [B2].*
*Tel: (212) 431-4646.*
*www.urbanarchaeology.com*
Once famous for salvaging furniture and fixtures from old houses, UA are now in the business of reproducing antique household items so you can buy them new. But they're always on the hunt for one-off original pieces from pool tables and juke boxes to shower heads and faucets.

# Electronics

### J&R
*23 Park Row [B3].*
*Tel: (212) 238-9000.*
*www.jr.com*
A gigantic string of stores selling every electronic item under the sun. J&R comprises a row of stores lined up along a whole block. Each has its own specific focus – audio/visual, household items, photography, music – and all guarantee unbeatable prices.

# Gifts & Souvenirs

### Mariposa: The Butterfly Gallery
*South Street Seaport,*
*Pier 17, 2nd Floor [C4].*
*Tel: (212) 233-3221.*
*www.mariposagallery.com*
The butterfly gallery sells beautiful and unusual arrangements as works of art. None of the butterflies used are endangered. They are bred on plantations and farms all over the world, expressly for lifetime preservation by Mariposa.

# Children

## Blue Bench

*159 Duane Street [B2].*
*Tel: (212) 267-1500.*
*www.bluebenchnyc.com*
If money is no object, parents will enjoy picking out furniture for their toddler's room or designing their baby's nursery. The quality hardwood furniture is handcrafted and painted with designs inspired by Folk Art.

## Boomerang Toys

*173 West Broadway [B2].*
*Tel: (212) 226-7650.*
*www.boomerangtoys.com*
Voted a Best Toy Store in New York City by Zagats, this store has everything from the expected, such as construction kits and bikes, to the fun and purely frivolous. And best of all, there is much to keep your children busy while you shop.
BRANCH: World Financial Center, 225 Liberty Street.

*Old-style suitcases and books for kids at Blue Bench.*

## Bu & the Duck

*106 Franklin Street [B2].*
*Tel: (212) 431-9226.*
*www.buandtheduck.com*
An old-fashioned feel pervades this store whose furnishings and clothing are vintage-inspired.

## Koh's Kids

*311 Greenwich Street [B2].*
*Tel: (212) 791-6915.*
A huge assortment of brand-named infant, toddler, and older kids' clothing, plus the owner's own line of hand-knitted items.

## Shoofly

*42 Hudson Street [B2].*
*Tel: (212) 406-3270.*
*www.shooflynyc.com*
Stylish shoes that are both funky and practical for your tots, plus a fun line of colorful hats and mittens.

# Food & Drink

## A.L. Bazzini

*339 Greenwich Street [B2].*
*Tel: (212) 334-1280.*
*www.bazzininuts.com*
This recently renovated specialty food shop stocks 24 different kinds of imported olive oil and many varieties of dried fruits and nuts. There is also a charcuterie counter.

## Godiva Chocolatier

*21 Fulton Street [C4].*
*Tel: (212) 571-6965.*
*www.godiva.com*
The purveyor of quality Belgian chocolates has several locations around the city; this one has the advantage of being situated in one of New York's oldest buildings.
BRANCHES: across Manhattan.

## Leonidas-Manon Cafe

*3 Hanover Square [B4].*
*Tel: (212) 422-9600.*
Get your chocolate to go or lounge around sipping coffee and nibbling chocolates in their cafe. A nice escape from the chaos outside.

# Specialist

### Balloon Saloon

*133 West Broadway [B2].*
*Tel: (212) 227-3838.*
*www.balloonsaloon.com*
Having a party? This quirky store sells balloons in all colors, shapes and sizes. Kids will love the animal range.

### Bowne & Company

*South Street Seaport Museum,*
*211 Water Street [C4].*
*Tel: (212) 748-8651.*
Bowne & Co specializes in custom-made stationery. Check out their historic printing equipment that has been in operation since the late 1800s.

### Pearl: Art, Craft & Graphic Discount Centers

*308 Canal Street [C2].*
*Tel: (212) 431-7932.*
*www.pearlpaint.com*
This store sells a similar range of stationery and paper goods to the better known Kate's Paperie *(see page 89)* but here it's at considerably lower prices. However, this store caters to an artist's needs - easels, brushes of all sizes, and canvases. There are other adjacent stores with specialist niches – crafts, framing, and paint.

### The Sharper Image

*Pier 17, 89 South Street [C4].*
*Tel: (212) 693-0477.*
*www.sharperimage.com*
Electric bikes, inflatable kayaks, hair removal kits, and all manner of gadgets to simplify one's life.
BRANCHES: 50 Rockefeller Plaza and 10 West 57th Street.

### Staples

*200 Water Street [C4].*
*Tel: (212) 785-9521.*
*www.staples.com*
If you need practical items such as pens, paper, storage boxes, envelopes, or computer accessories, there are a slew of branches around Manhattan for you to pop into and stock up.

### Tents and Trails

*21 Park Place [B3].*
*Tel: (212) 227-1760.*
*www.tenttrails.com*
Tents and Trails three-story building is packed to the rafters with tents, hiking boots, ski shells, and pretty much anything campers and outdoor adventurers might need – all at reasonable, mostly discounted prices.

*Top: Blue Bench is known for its high quality toys and children's furniture.*

*Lunch at one of South Street Seaport's restaurants.*

## WHERE TO UNWIND

### Bubble Lounge
*228 West Broadway [B2]*
*Tel: (212) 431-3433*
If you want to 'toast' your purchases, you can sit for hours in this champagne lounge and nibble on caviar.

### New York Water Taxi
*Pier 16, South Street Seaport [C4]. Tel: (212) 742-1969 x 0. www.nywatertaxi.com*
There are two downtown locations to pick up the New York Water Taxi – Battery Park and South Street Seaport. The 'taxi' can take you on a tour of the waterways or you can use it as a means of transportation around the city or to Brooklyn. Tickets required and the schedule in the winter months is reduced.

### Columbine
*229 West Broadway [B2]. Tel: (212) 965-0909. www.columbine229.com*
Columbine does fresh juices, sandwiches, and pastries to keep you nourished while you shop.

### Fraunces Tavern
*54 Pearl Street [B5]. Tel: (212) 968-1776.*
*www.frauncestavern.com*
This historical landmark has a restaurant downstairs, which specializes in American cuisine, and a museum upstairs. The building is famous for housing George Washington during his tenure as president. There is often live jazz in the evenings.

### South Street Seaport
*Pier 17 [C4]. Tel: (212) Seaport.*
*www.southstreetseaport.com*
In the Seaport Mall there are a handful of restaurants, all of which charge for the great views they offer, and a cheap food court, where you can stand and eat or fight for one of the few tables. In warmer weather it's great to sit outside and take it all in.

### Ula Day Spa
*8 Harrison Street [B2]. Tel: (212) 343-2376.*
*www.tribecabeautyspa.com*
Treat yourself to any number of massages, facials, waxings, or even a $15 manicure just so that you can soak up the atmosphere at this calming and unpretentious spot. Perfect post-shopping relaxation.

# Discount Stores

*As well as offering the shopper unrivaled glamour and choice,*
*New York also caters to the bargain hunter*

To most people, the appeal of shopping in New York City is in large part due to the profusion of specialty shops, the one-of-a-kind designers, those upscale stores you otherwise read about only in glossy magazines. It's inarguable that the city offers the best of everything, at prices we are supposed to be willing to bear for the high quality or sheer thrill of making such a purchase.

But this isn't the full picture. New York may be one of the most expensive places to shop in America, but it also offers some of its best bargains. Sample sales are launched almost every day, and warehouse clearance sales are equally common; these things you have to hunt for, learn about from those fliers thrust at you on the street, or read about in *New York Magazine*. There are also bargains to be had at the numerous street vendors (on Canal Street, for example) and at flea markets and street fairs *(see page 57)*.

On the other hand, there are always those shops created to serve bargain hunters on a daily basis. Discount shopping has long been synonymous with Filene's Basement and Loehmann's *(see pages 42 and 52)*, both of which were Boston landmarks before branching into New York several years ago. However, New York has discount shops of its own: Bolton's, Syms, Daffy's, Strawberry's, Century 21, and Conway's, amongst others. All of these stores have more than one location throughout New York City, and most have several branches. What's in stock depends on what has been cleared out from the previous season's selections from department stores and other places that are feeding grounds for these discount operations. Not all items are hand-me-downs from other stores, as some stock their own brands or have non-brand name versions of what is otherwise considered designer clothing. The items, mostly clothing and household goods, are a little picked over, with some looking downright used, but you're likely to forgive these flaws for the bargain prices available.

*Discounted perfumes on Canal Street.*

# BROOKLYN

*When Manhattan's prices soared as high as its buildings, Brooklyn became fashionable. But it still clings to its individuality*

**B**rooklyn is two-and-a-half times the size of Manhattan, and when it comes to population, only a handful of American cities exceed the borough across the East River. Sure, Manhattan has all the glamour, though if you want a really good view of the famous New York skyline you have to go over to Brooklyn to get it. Aside from its own denizens, Brooklyn has always attracted a certain number of Manhattanites for various reasons, like lower rents, and in the mid-1990s a lot more defected via bridge and tunnel to the other side. They could no longer afford to live in Manhattan, where the Internet and Silicon Alley were all the rage, rents were spiraling, stores were charging as much as $150 for white T-shirts, and cigar and champagne bars were almost as common as hot dog vendors. Priced out by all this conspicuous consumption, people removed themselves to Brooklyn, where the main lures were Park Slope and Brooklyn Heights. These areas in turn became fully secured as yuppie neighborhoods, with fancy town houses, latte cafés and a range of bookstores, jewelry shops, and a few fashion boutiques. Today, these areas have gone the way of most of Manhattan, importing their stores rather than sustaining local businesses, being dependent on mass manufacturing, and being similar rather than different.

## Moving On Up

With the gentrification of these neighborhoods, new bohemian areas sprung up to take their place – examples being Williamsburg, DUMBO, Fort Greene, Red Hook, and the triumvirate of **Bo**erum Hill, **Co**bble Hill, and **Ca**rroll Gardens that is billing itself for marketing purposes as Bococa. It could be said that Brooklyn has come into its own. DUMBO (yet another acronym; **d**own **u**nder the **M**anhattan **B**ridge **O**verpass) and Williamsburg, like Soho before them, began as artist's colonies – and the stores reflected this, as they always do. Now these once-cheap lofts have been refurbished as expensive apartments.

*Opposite: Layla sells handmade Indian items. Below: Stylish tableware at Bark.*

Stores have developed to cater to new residents and inspire others to make the trek to Brooklyn, and in their wake have followed restaurants and cultural events. These neighborhoods are the way others in Manhattan and Brooklyn used to be, and most people hope they can sustain this niche.

Of course, there are numerous other neighborhoods in Brooklyn, too, serving mostly low- to moderate-income New Yorkers, and many have long-standing immigrant communities. For the adventurous shopper, these sections of New York are great to explore. They promise little in terms of high-end shopping, but if you want interesting ethnic foods or

clothing, or you can't or don't want to afford the prices in the more popular shopping areas, there's no end to the exploring you can do.

## Mixed Feelings

*Right:*
*Looking*
*towards*
*Manhattan*
*from Brooklyn*
*Heights.*

Living in the shadow of Manhattan has made Brooklyn's residents outspoken (or defensive) about their borough and what it has to offer. One almost feels there is a Brooklyn public-relations campaign going on – witness the sweatshirts stamped 'Brooklyn' advertising all that awaits you in the borough. However, this desire to talk up the area, and to convince Manhattanites and others to visit, is tempered by the wish to prevent the mall-ification and soaring rents that previously down-to-earth parts of Manhattan have experienced. The familiar fear is that once other stores realize how successful the shopping has become in Brooklyn, bigger businesses will move in and force local ones out. What can help to preserve the happy status quo is simultaneous pressure and support from shoppers.

## Crossing Over

Brooklyn appears much farther away than it is. Most of the popular areas are one to three subway stops into Brooklyn – and for anyone coming from Lower Manhattan, it's actually a quicker trip here than it is to Upper Manhattan. There is also easy access to Williamsburg, provided by the Williamsburg

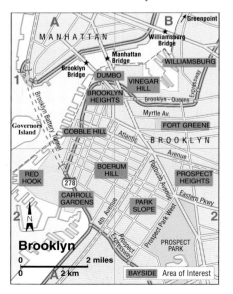

Bridge, and to DUMBO and Brooklyn Heights, which are both at the foot of the Brooklyn Bridge. Taxi drivers know the neighborhoods, even if they balk at taking you there – and the walk across any of the bridges is refreshing. (See *Local Attractions*, for more on crossing the Brooklyn Bridge.)

Out of all four "outer" boroughs, Brooklyn is the most happening. The listings in this chapter cover its main neighborhoods, DUMBO, Park Slope, Williamsburg and BoCoCa (Boerum Hill, Cobble Hill and Carroll Gardens). These are just four of Brooklyn's two dozen or so districts, but rapid development means that neighborhood boundaries are beginning to blur. There are many up-and-coming areas to be discovered, such as Greenpoint and Vinegar Hill. Shopping tends to be concentrated on one street – in Park

Slope you can stick to 7th Avenue and increasingly 5th, in DUMBO pretty much everything intersects with Front Street, while Atlantic Avenue is awash with great shops. Park Slope is one of the more established neighborhoods, so in addition to small boutiques you will find chains like the Gap, Starbucks and Barnes and Noble. Arty Williamsburg is centred around Bedford Avenue and has a proliferation of galleries, edgy bars and cafes, and a large Hasidic community. *Brooklyn Now,* available at www.BrooklynNow.com and in many stores, can give you up-to-the-minute information about what to find in a given neighborhood.

## LOCAL ATTRACTIONS

**Brooklyn Bridge** is the main thoroughfare into Brooklyn, which you can – and should – walk across. It gives you a great view over four boroughs (you can't see the Bronx), and of the Statue of Liberty. In the tower on the Brooklyn side you might catch an art exhibit or other cultural event.

The bridge leads you to the **Brooklyn Promenade**, for a stroll with a view of Manhattan, and into DUMBO, Brooklyn's riverside area, an artists' enclave after soaring rents forced them to leave Manhattan. The **Brooklyn Museum of Art** and the **Brooklyn Botanical Gardens** are both a short subway ride away. In summer you can swim in the floating pool.

## Charm and Quality

In Brooklyn, as in Nolita in Manhattan, it's common to find a shop owner working in the store and for some of the goods to be made on site or nearby. Another similarity is that most shop owners are supportive of their neighbors, and overall the area has the same community feel that gives Nolita so much warmth and character. And just as many of Nolita's stores are run by first-time store owners having a go at running their own business, so too are those in Brooklyn. Some even share space – cutting costs and drumming up business for each other. The range of stores in these areas is just as complete as in any other neighborhood – though you do have fewer choices within each type of store. Some would argue that this means you're being offered better quality.

If you have time, you should definitely try to fit Brooklyn into your shopping trip. It makes a pleasant break from Manhattan, and is one of the most diverse parts of New York. It will make you feel good to know you're supporting these emerging businesses. You're also likely to get a good deal, and walk away with something unique that no one else will have – one of the main reasons people come to shop in New York City in the first place.

*Across the Great Divide on the Brooklyn Bridge.*

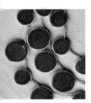

# Fashion & Footwear

### Bird
*430 Seventh Avenue (Park Slope). Tel: (718) 768-4940. www.shopbird.com*
This store is symbolic of the unique style and choices of most Brooklyn boutiques. Here you find women's clothing and accessory items you haven't seen a dozen times. A personal shopper of sorts.
BRANCH: 220 Smith Street, Cobble Hill, Brooklyn.

### Brooklyn Industries
*206 Fifth Avenue (Park Slope). Tel: (718) 789-2764. www.brooklynindustries.com*
Run by a young urban couple, this label epitomizes urban fashion – bleak, practical, and sturdy. Their bags and coats are what mostly draw people in, but there are other clothing staples for men and women.

### Butter
*389 Atlantic Avenue (BoCoCa). Tel: (718) 260-9033.*
Butter does a small selection of women's clothes and shoes. Most of the cool designers represented, are found in department stores, but this store carries a choice of their sharpest items.

### Diane T.
*174 Court Street (BoCoCa). Tel: (718) 923-5777*
The women's clothes and shoes here are consistent with what you will find at any hip women's clothing store, but the accessories give Diane T. the edge.

### Flirt
*93 Fifth Avenue (Park Slope). Tel: (718) 783-0364. www.flirt-brooklyn.com*
BRANCH: 252 Smith Street, (BoCoCa).

Flirt stocks new clothes made with vintage or used fabrics. The styles are simple, but unique; most are produced by local designers. They even teach onsite home-ec courses to brush up on your sewing.

### Jumelle
*148 Bedford Avenue, (Williamsburg). Tel: (718) 388-9525. www.shopjumelle.com*
Delicate and sweet women's fashions, clothing that drapes your body and is sure to make you feel special.

### Kimera
*366 Atlantic Avenue (BoCoCa). Tel: (718) 422-1147.*
Selling a mixture of items such as handmade silk pillow cases and quilted jackets, this is a good place to outfit yourself and your home.

### Layla
*86 Hoyt Street (BoCoCa). Tel: (718) 222-1933*
Pretty shop selling handmade Indian scarves, clothing, and accessories. The owner handpicks most of the range.

### Melting Pot
*492 Atlantic Avenue (BoCoCa). Tel: (718) 596-6849*
This store exclusively sells Batik clothing, for men, women, and children. There are some great designs.

*Layla's handmade Indian designs.*

### Zoe

*68 Washington Street (Williamsburg). Tel: (718) 237-4002. www.shopzoeonline.com*
A full range of high-end women's fashion – most brand name designers and a few unique items. The range is impressive for a small store.

## Jewelry & Accessories

### Catbird

*390 Metropolitan Avenue (Williamsburg). Tel: (718) 388-7688. www.catbirdnyc.com*
Prioritizing women's jewelry, this tiny shop exudes femininity. Though the offers are luxurious, the prices are fair.
BRANCH: 219 Bedford Avenue, Williamsburg.

### The Clay Pot

*162 Seventh Avenue (Park Slope). Tel: (718) 625-6005. www.clay-pot.com*
A long-time favorite for couples looking for wedding rings. This store sells popular styles and designs, but more so items that appear to be made just for you – and sometimes are.

### Debbie Fisher Jewelry

*461 Court Street (BoCoCa). Tel: (718) 625-6005*
Debbie Fisher sells handmade jewelry, using colorful stones and gems. Most designs are strung together with silver.

## Health & Beauty

### The HomeSpa

*300 Court Street (BoCoCa). Tel: (718) 596-8668*
This laid-back store, which is related to Blissful Botanicals on Bergen Street, sells soaps, bath salts, and other bath products.

## Design & Interiors

### Circa Antiques Ltd

*377 Atlantic Avenue (BoCoCa). Tel: (718) 596-1866*
The antiques here – from practical kitchen chairs to decorative flower boxes – date from the 19th century.

### City Foundry

*365 Atlantic Avenue (BoCoCa). Tel: (718) 923-1786*
It's hard to determine when 'used' ends and 'antique' begins, but these functional items will add an individual touch to home or office.

### Kea Carpets & Kilims

*477 Atlantic Avenue (BoCoCa). Tel: (718) 222-8087*
A great selection of Indian and Turkish kilims is offered here – all at far more reasonable prices than those you will find in Manhattan.

**TIP**
The majority of Brooklyn's stores are only open on weekends, or Wednesday through Sunday, so you're best advised to visit on one of these days.

*Breakfast at
Bar Tabac.*

**TIP**
If you choose to take a taxi, note that Brooklyn has its own taxi system – Manhattan cabs can only pick you up from that borough. To catch a cab in Brooklyn, you need to call ahead – shops and restaurants should be able to recommend a cab firm.

### Michael Anchin Glass

*51 South 1st Street
(Williamsburg). Tel: (212) 925-
1470. www.michaelanchin.com*
Colorful blown glass lamps and
vases on sale at the artist's studio.

### Rico

*384 Atlantic Avenue (BoCoCa).
Tel: (718) 797-2077*
Its quality and range make Rico
look more like a gallery than a
design store. Homeware from
lampshades to furniture.

### Silk Road Antiques

*313 Atlantic Avenue (BoCoCa).
Tel: (718) 802-9500*
Antiques from China and other
parts of Asia. Be sure to take a peek
at the beautiful garden in the back.

### West Elm

*75 Front Street (DUMBO).
Tel: (718) 875-7757*
The West Elm catalogue of
reasonably priced homewares and
contemporary furniture is now
opening stores across the US.

## Books & Music

### Halcyon

*57 Pearl Street (DUMBO).
Tel: (718) 260-9299*
Halycon is part record store, design
boutique and gallery. If you want
hipness – here it is – slightly intimidating for those just browsing.

## Food & Drink

### Bedford Cheese Shop

*229 Bedford Avenue (Williams-
burg). Tel: (718) 599-7588.
www.bedfordcheeseshop.com*
Buyer beware, it's hard to resist
the delicious cheeses and their
beautiful display. The range of this
relatively small shop matches that
of the larger stores, but here you
can actually ask questions and
sample the goods without feeling
too pressed for by your fellow
shoppers.

## Children

### Acorn

*323 Atlantic Avenue (BoCoCa).
Tel: (718) 522-3760.
wwwqcorntoyshop.com*
Solid wooden toys are this store's
specialty, catering mostly to
younger children, toddlers and
infants. Run by parents, the store is
parent approved and kid friendly.

### The Green Onion

*274 Smith Street (BoCoCa).
Tel: (718) 246-2804*
This children's clothing store
stocks items that will go down a
treat with bohemian parents.

### Gumbo

*493 Atlantic Avenue (BoCoCa).
Tel: (718) 855-7808*

Come here for basic and ethnic-style children's clothes. At weekends the store hosts programs for kids, such as puppetry and music.

**Pomme**
*81 Washington Street (DUMBO).*
*Tel: (718) 855-0623.*
*www.pommenyc.com*
The French name is a hint of the European designs and labels that await you at this childrens store.

# Specialist

**Bark**
*495 Atlantic Avenue (BoCoCa).*
*Tel: (718) 625-8997*
Pamper yourself with beautiful lingerie, fine French soaps, and silky smooth Indian sheets.

**A Cook's Companion**
*197 Atlantic Avenue (BoCoCa).*
*Tel: (718) 852-6901*
Need a bagel slicer? This kitchenware store stocks a wide range of utensils for the kitchen, both practical and obscure.

**Refinery**
*254 Smith Street (BoCoCa).*
*Tel: (718) 643-7861*
A quirky shop selling bags made of vintage fabrics and cotton baseball T-shirts with funky logos, such as '718,' the Brooklyn area code.

**Salvation Army Thrift Shop**
*180 Bedford Avenue (Williamsburg). Tel: (718) 388-9249.*
There are countless thrift shops around New York, all carrying a random assortment of used goods, from bicycles to lamps, and china to clothing, but this charity seems to acquire better quality wares than your average second-hand store. Good for a rummage.

**Zoe Papers**
*315 Atlantic Avenue (BoCoCa).*
*Tel: (718) 625-5797*
Beautiful handmade paper is on display here along with photo albums, journals, stationery, cards and personalized invitations. Their handmade wrapping paper will make any present desirable.

## WHERE TO UNWIND

**Bar Tabac**
*128 Smith Street (BoCoCa).*
*Tel: (718) 923-0918. www.bartabacny.com*
This bar would look quite at home in the arty Marais quarter of Paris. In warm weather the floor-to-ceiling doors are left open.

**Brawta Caribbean Café**
*347 Atlantic Avenue (BoCoCa).*
*Tel: (718) 855-5515. www.brawtacafe.com*
People come from all over for this taste of the Caribbean. Justifiably famed jerk chicken.

**Marlow and Sons**
*81 Broadway (Williamsburg). Tel: (718) 384-1441. www.marlowandsons.com*
Duck into this food shop and discover a complete restaurant in the back, with an ever-changing menu. You can soak up the ambiance

or relax at one of their outdoor tables and take in the laid-back Brooklyn atmosphere, while getting a glimpse of Manhattan with the subway rattling by.

**River Café**
*1 Water Street (DUMBO/Brooklyn Heights).*
*Tel: (718) 522-5200. www.rivercafe.com*
Housed in a converted coffee barge is one of New York's fanciest restaurants. You can stop by for a drink, although it won't be cheap.

**St. Ann's Warehouse**
*38 Water Street, DUMBO [A1]. Tel: (718) 254-8779. www.stannswarehouse.org*
Call ahead to find out what avant-garde theater or musical event is happening at this beautifully restored spice milling factory-cum-performance space.

# ESSENTIAL INFORMATION

Here is our low-down on transport, money, opening times and when to find that top bargain in the sales. For further practical tips, contact the Tourist Information service *(see below)*; for useful New York listings, pick up the weekly magazines *The New Yorker, New York*, or *Time Out New York*

## Money Matters

Foreign exchange offices are relatively few and far between in New York, and many banks lack exchange facilities. Branches of Chase Manhattan bank, as well as Thomas Cook and American Express offices, will exchange foreign currencies. Major credit cards are accepted by most shops and restaurants, and can be used to withdraw cash from ATMs. Large hotels will exchange money, but offer poor rates.

## Tipping

It is the norm to tip. A tip of around 15 to 20 percent is usual for waiters, bartenders, and hairdressers. Taxi drivers generally expect around $1, or around 15 percent of the fare if it is over $10. Porters usually get $1 per bag.

## Opening Hours

Each shopping area tends to have slightly different opening times – the general rule is that downtown stores open and close an hour or two later than uptown. Most department stores and many other shops open 10am–6pm Monday–Saturday, with evening hours on Thursdays. Some stay open until 8pm or 9pm and are also open on Sundays.

## Public Holidays

1 January (New Year's Day); Third Monday in January (Martin Luther King Day); Third Monday in February (President's Day); Last Monday in May (Memorial Day); 4 July (Independence Day); First Monday in September (Labor Day); Second Monday in October (Columbus Day); 11 November (Veterans' Day); Last Thursday in November (Thanksgiving); 25 December (Christmas Day).

## Public Transport

New York's **subways** and **buses** operate 24 hours. The $2.00 fare is payable on any journey, no matter how far you are traveling. Various travel passes valid for 1, 7 or 30 days are also available. For information call (718) 330 1234. For lost property call (212) 712 4500.

## To/From the Airports

Public transport links between Manhattan and New York's three airports are indirect and slow. The best option is to take a private bus (typically around $15–20) or a taxi (a flat rate of $45 from or to JFK).

## Refunds

Refund policies are best at the larger stores, where a full refund can typically be received within 30 days of purchase. Smaller stores may only exchange goods or give credit towards another purchase *(see Tip, page 22.)*

## Sales

The best months for sales in New York are January and July, as well as immediately after Christmas. Many stores also run sales on or around public holidays *(see Tip, page 20.)*

## Taxis

Manhattan taxis can be hailed in the street. When the middle light on the roof is switched on, the taxi is available. Get in before telling the driver where you want to go. When the outer lights are on, the driver is off duty – this usually happens between the hours of 4 and 6 pm. If no lights are on, the taxi is occupied. There are a few official taxi ranks, mainly at transport hubs such as Grand Central Station. Between 4 and 8pm there is a $1 surcharge on all taxi rides.

## Telephones

The area code for Manhattan is 212 or 646; for other parts of the city the code is 718 or 347. Toll-free calls are prefixed by 800, 888, and 877. Remember to dial 1 first when calling these numbers, and when calling from one area code to another. You must dial an area code even when dialing within the area code. The international dialling code for the US is also 1. Emergencies: 911. Directory assistance: 411. Public payphones take all silver coins and are increasingly hard to find around Manhattan; the best network to use is Verizon. For long distance calls use AT&T, Sprint, or MCI. The favored wireless networks to use are Verizon, AT&T and TMobile.

## Tourist Information

New York City's official visitor information center is at 810 Seventh Avenue, between 52nd & 53rd Streets, open Monday–Friday 8.30am–6pm, Saturday & Sunday 9am–5pm. Dial 311 in New York to get all kinds of information and to be connected to the relevant department, for instance if you are seeking information on parking rules or garbage rules.

## Sales Tax

There is an 8.375 percent sales tax but prescription drugs, some clothing and footwear and non-prepared food bought in grocery stores are exempt from this. Check the website nyc.gov for details.

Non US residents are entitled to tax free purchases of articles up to $100 in value for use as gifts, if they remain in the US for at least 72 hours. This exemption or any part of it can be claimed only once every six months. Up to 100 cigars can be included, but alcoholic beverages are excluded. Don't have articles gift wrapped, as they must be available for customs inspection.

## Websites

Two good sites for what's on listings are www.newyork.citysearch.com and www.newyorktoday.com. For background information, visit www.nycvisit.com.

Editorial
*Project Editor*  Tom Le Bas
*Series Editor*  Cathy Muscat
*Editorial Director*  Brian Bell
*Art Director*  Klaus Geisler
*Design*  Tanvir Virdee
*Update*  Scarlett O'Hara, Paula Soper
*Picture Manager*  Hilary Genin
*Photographer*  Mark Read
All Pictures © APA/ Mark Read except; Alamy Cover, 5ML, 65T; Corbis 2B, 66BL; Getty 3B, 4, 5T, 98
Distribution
*UK & Ireland*
GeoCenter International Ltd
Meridian House, Churchill Way West, Basingstoke, Hampshire, RG21 6YR Tel: (44 1256) 817 987
*United States*
Langenscheidt Publishers, Inc.
36-36 33rd Street, 4th Floor, Long Island City, New York, 11106 Tel: (1 718) 784 0055
*Australia*
Universal Publishers
1 Waterloo Road, Macquarie Park, NSW 2113
Fax: (61) 2 9888 9074
*New Zealand*
Hema Maps New Zealand Ltd (HNZ)
Unit D, 24 Ra ORA Drive, East Tamaki, Auckland
Fax: (64) 9 273 6479
*Worldwide*
Apa Publications GmbH & Co.

Verlag KG (Singapore branch)
38 Joo Koon Road, Singapore 628990
Tel: (65) 6865-1600. Fax: (65) 6861-6438
Printing
Insight Print Services (Pte) Ltd
38 Joo Koon Road, Singapore 628990
Tel: (65) 6865-1600. Fax: (65) 6861-6438

©2008  Apa Publications GmbH & Co.
Verlag KG (Singapore branch)
*All Rights Reserved*
*First Edition 2003 (Updated 2008)*
CONTACTING THE EDITORS

www.insightguides.com

# SHOPS A–Z

The following is a complete list of the shops reviewed in this guide and where to find them. For details of other branches refer to the main entry – where these are too numerous to list in full, a general enquiries number for the store has been given.

## Fashion & Footwear

# Health & Beauty

# Department Stores

# Design & Interiors

## Books, Music, & Electronics

## Specialist

**Acknowledgments**
The publishers would like to thank all stores kind
enough to allow us to photograph on their premises.